Forward to Teach

Forward to Teach

by Francis V. Lloyd, Jr.

Illustrated by John Gretzer

LITTLE, BROWN AND COMPANY

BOSTON

TORONTO

The author wishes to thank the following for their kind permission to quote from books, articles, papers, reports, and speeches:

Rose Bello for a passage on "Listening" from a report for The Laboratory Schools, The University of Chicago.

Faber and Faber, Ltd., publishers, for a passage from *Good Enough for the Children?* by John Blackie.

Patrick Bratton for the poem "Song on a Spring Day to Miss K."

Harvard University Press for a passage from *The Process of Education* by Jerome Bruner, 1963.

Prentice-Hall, Inc. for a passage from *Improving the Teaching of Reading* by Emerald V. Dechant. © 1964.

Kappa Delta Pi, An Honor Society in Education (owners of the copyright), for passages from *Experience and Education* by John Dewey, 1928. Published by The Macmillan Company.

John A. Downing, Scott, Foresman & Company, and the University of London Institute of Education for material from *The i.t.a. Reading Experiment* by John A. Downing.

William Fowler for a passage from the Minutes of the Department of Counseling and Guidance, May 4, 1965, The Laboratory Schools, The University of Chicago.

Harper & Row, Publishers, for passages from *The Child from Five to Ten* by Arnold Gesell and Frances Ilg, 1946.

W. W. Norton & Company, Inc., for a passage from *The Greek Way* by Edith Hamilton.

McGraw-Hill Book Company for a passage from *Educating Emotionally Disturbed Children* by N. G. Haring and E. L. Phillips, 1962.

Philip Jackson for passages from his paper "Educational Objectives and the Joys of Teaching."

Educational Testing Service for a statement by John Gardner quoted in "Learning to Read," a report published by Educational Testing Service, New Jersey, in 1962, based upon a conference held in New York City, September, 1961.

The Philosophical Library, Inc. for a passage from *Yankee Teacher* by Kurt F. Leidecker, 1946.

G. P. Putnam's Sons for a passage from *Fives at School* by Elenora Haegele Moore, 1959.

Congressman William S. Moorehead for a passage from his speech "For the Establishment of a National Foundation for the Humanities," delivered before the deans of the graduate schools of the Association of State Universities and Land-Grant Colleges, November 9, 1964.

Robert E. Newman for a passage from his article "A Book Is to Buy," published in the *Saturday Review*, January 16, 1965.

Eleanor C. Parker for a passage from a statement to the School Board of Laconia, New Hampshire.

Morvin A. Wirtz for a passage from a letter from him to Francis V. Lloyd, Jr.

We have been unable to locate Dr. Samuel Boorstein for permission to quote from his book *Orthopedics for the Teachers of Crippled Children,* published by the Aidem Publishing Co., New York, 1935, and would be grateful for any information which might enable us to obtain proper clearance.

To Betty, my beloved wife,
mother of our three sons,
and Molly,
our daughter, an elementary
teacher trainee

Introduction

IN THIS BOOK there is an attempt to give in considerable detail the practical answers as to what opportunities exist for someone wishing to be an elementary school teacher, and how to go about training oneself to be an elementary teacher. There is also an attempt to give an understanding and a "feeling" of what it is really like to teach young children. It is more possible to give *all* the practical answers as to how to become a teacher than it is possible to re-create *all* the feelings that teachers have.

I commend to the readers the Bibliography, which has been chosen with great care to be representative of the best writing and of the best research. It is intended to supplement in depth what has been written in this short book. Reading from the list in any area in which you are interested should give you greater insight and understanding.

This book has been fun to write. If at times what is written seems on the romantic side, you are right. I find teaching, and particularly teaching young children, very romantic. If at times what is written appears to be harsh, you are right again. There are many conditions in education today that need to be handled better, where the child is being sacrificed to all sorts of interests and considerations which are not related to his welfare. Teaching is not wholly romantic nor is it totally harsh. It is hoped that what has been written in this book is close to the truth, a picture of "real" teaching. It is hoped that having read it you will want to consider teaching as your way of contributing to society, and your choice for self-fulfillment. Teaching is gay and exciting. It is somber and hard. Done well it is more rewarding than any other way of life.

FRANCIS V. LLOYD, JR.

The Laboratory Schools
The University of Chicago

Contents

Forward to Teach

1 Those Who Dare to Teach Must Never Cease to Learn

THESE were some of the rules for teachers in New York City in 1872:

(1) Teachers each day will fill lamps, clean chimneys and trim the wicks.

(2) Each teacher will bring a bucket of water and scuttle of coal for the day's session.

(3) Make your pens carefully. You may whittle nibs to the individual taste of the pupil.

(4) Men teachers may take one evening each week for courting purposes, or two evenings if they go to church regularly.

(5) After ten hours of school, the teacher should spend the remaining time reading the Bible or other good books.

(6) Women teachers who marry or engage in unseemly conduct will be dismissed.

(7) Every teacher should lay aside from each pay a goodly sum of his earnings for his benefit during his declining years so that he will not become a burden to society.

(8) Any teacher who smokes, uses liquors in any form, frequents pool or other public halls or gets shaved in a barber shop, will give good reason to suspect his worth, intentions, integrity and honesty.

(9) That teacher who performs his labors faithfully and without fault for five years will be given an increase of 25¢ per week in his pay provided the Board of Education approves.

Conditions have changed greatly for the better in the last hundred years! Today teaching is considered a profession. As professionals, teachers are required to be trained in the same manner that society requires doctors, lawyers, architects, and engineers to be trained.

There are a number of different ways of being trained as an elementary school teacher. To start with, you need enthusiasm, an urge to be creative, a love of children, an inquiring mind, a desire to go on learning, physical health, optimism, and a sense of humor. No one person has all these qualities in equal quantities. Some of them may be latent, or dormant; in other words, you may not know that you have them but they may be revealed under certain circumstances. Don't be discouraged from attempting to train as an elementary teacher just because you do not see yourself as possessing ideal qualifications. If all the signs are negative, on the other hand, it might be foolish to spend time preparing yourself to be a teacher. But you cannot tell whether you will enjoy teaching or be a good teacher until you actually try it.

Training is necessary. Anything worth learning takes time to learn, and time to teach. People are not born teachers any more than they are born doctors or born engineers. Teaching is not totally an art if by that is meant it is instinctive, intuitive. Teaching requires discipline of the mind; teaching requires intensive training. It is degrading to teachers as professionals to suggest that anyone can teach, that it requires no special qualities and requires no special training. Elementary teachers particularly, since so much is asked of them, need a broad and rich training. If a doctor has not had enough training, the results of his lack of knowledge are almost immediately apparent. Sometimes those results are even tragic. No one would dream of entrusting himself to a doctor who had only a couple of years of medical school and no internship. The effects of bad teaching, although sometimes immediately visible, oftentimes are not apparent until years later.

This fact has permitted people to excuse bad teaching, to overlook it, and in fact in some cases to deprecate and even to ridicule the necessity for intensive and disciplined training for teachers. Sadly enough, the teaching profession itself has not done enough to promote the dignity of teachers. All too seldom in the past has the profession emphasized the need for quality, the necessity of standards. Happily, this general attitude is changing and changing rapidly.

Most states by law now require that public school teachers have at least four years of training in a recognized college or university. Most states by law have spelled out a minimum number of courses that must be taken during the training period to qualify an individual for certification. Most states by law require some form of practice teaching or internship before an individual is allowed to teach in a public school classroom. So-called certification requirements have not always been wisely selected or administered. Even though in some states change and progress is painfully slow, the trend across the country is for a clearer and better understanding of what courses and experiences are truly essential for the beginning teacher. States are now stripping away and eliminating those courses and experiences which are of doubtful value.

As so often happens, the pendulum had swung from an extreme of almost no required training to the equally extreme position which specified courses of such narrow design that they lacked any intellectual content. Faced with such requirements, many intelligent and sensitive people decided that they were not going into teaching. Today a sensible compromise appears to have been established.

Teachers must be trained sensibly and realistically to understand existing conditions. The tremendous increase in number of school-age children requires hundreds of thousands of new teachers; and the unbelievable increase in new knowledge requires greater training and education of teachers at all levels. Furthermore, even at the lowest level of labor, skills and understanding undreamed of only twenty years ago are necessities. All of these problems must be faced and solved if our way of life is to survive.

Any nation which does not make its people literate, which does not provide its people with a chance to understand the fundamentals of our technological age, which does not train people in the necessary skills to carry on life as it now exists, will disappear. Who leads in the nuclear bomb race has terrifying and immediate significance. But for the future, so long as no one chooses to toss the bomb, peace, security, and growth will be possible only if day by day victories are achieved in individual classrooms throughout our country. And these must be elementary classrooms. If the job isn't done properly by teachers in the pre-school and primary grades, the high school, college and university teachers can never catch up. There simply isn't the time left. If reading isn't properly taught and if an understanding of the relationship of numbers is not given to each child, no amount of brilliance at research institutes or graduate schools in great universities can compensate for these basic lacks. The most challenging, the most exciting frontier today can be found in the elementary classroom.

Never before in our country has the need been greater for trained elementary teachers. In 1965 the United States Office of Education stated that there were close to 36 million children enrolled in elementary schools, 10 million more than in 1956. This was an average gain of a million elementary school children a year. During the same period of ten years the number of elementary teachers increased from 850,000 to 1,128,000, an average growth of 27,400 a year. Despite these large numbers the United States does not have enough trained elementary teachers. Many more young people are needed as teachers.

In the United States we have always had a dream that all the people should receive an adequate education, an education that would give their talents full development. As in dreams, the focus has never been sharp or clear. Certain parts of our great country interpreted this dream in one way; other regions of the country in ways far different. Within each state, as rural and urban areas made demands, there were differences of emphasis on what was needed to fulfill the dream. Even within a single big city there were inequalities. The nation still believed that every child did have an equal educational opportunity. We would say, "Of course, every child is not equal in ability but at least in the United States each individual has an equal chance to gain an education, to better himself and to become a full-fledged citizen."

This sentimental belief, for unfortunately that's all it was, was bolstered by our belief in "local control" of public schools. That is to say, each community decided for itself what kind of quality it wished to have in the education of the children of its community. Each state decided for itself what the overall goals would be and set minimum standards to attain them. As a nation we said and still say (although less emphatically today) that we wanted no part of Federal planning, control, or interference.

Under the great pressures and frighteningly brilliant light of world events most people woke up to the fact that we were not giving every child an equal opportunity. In fact, we were denying hundreds of thousands of children throughout the country — in the North, in the South, in the East, and in the West — the chance of preparing themselves even to a minimum degree for the world that existed about them and for a world that obviously was making increasing demands day by day upon every individual. It took a world crisis to make us face up to our inadequacies. We are a long, long way from meeting all our needs. What was a dream to be obtained some day has now become an immediate and stark necessity.

In a small town in northern New England, whose town limits border the most prosperous city in the state, the only public school facilities available to the children are housed in a three-story building constructed at the turn of the century. Grades one through four are on the first floor, five through eight on the second floor and nine through twelve on the third floor. Each of these floors has one teacher and one of the three teachers also serves as principal of the school. Only a mile away in the school district of the city can be found a modern elementary school with an average of twenty-five children to a classroom. Each class has not only a homeroom teacher, but also special teachers in physical education, music, and art. The high schools of this city are equipped with the most modern libraries, science laboratories, home economics and shop facilities, language laboratories, and physical education facilities. The average salaries of the city's teachers are almost double the average salaries of the three teachers in the small-town school.

The power of the state board of education in this state is almost nonexistent. There are permissive laws for the merger of poorer districts but they are not mandatory. The citizens of the city are reluctant to take on a school district whose tax base is low and which therefore would be a drag on them. And, ironically enough, the citizens of the village are reluctant to join with the big city since they claim they do not want to lose their identity as a community. The victims of these adult considerations and prejudices are the children — the future citizens of the United States.

Other states have faced the situation more realistically. New York and California, for instance, have set minimum standards below which no town can slip. But even in these great states the differences of opportunities for children are far too many.

Until a few years ago many Southern states thought there could be separate but equal schools for people of different races. It took the Supreme Court of the United States to rectify this situation. The Southern states were not only failing to provide equal opportunities in their dual school systems but because of the dual school systems and the extra cost involved they were depriving all children of all races opportunities that children in the rest of the country enjoyed.

In too many of our big cities where immigration from rural areas has overcrowded the schools it is still believed that, to be fair, equal amounts of money should be spent in each of the schools regardless of their needs. This is exactly like saying that we will spend exactly the same amount of money on the foundations and footings for each of three different buildings, one to be built on sand, one on granite, and one on marshy land. It is clear what would happen. The building built on sand would topple over after a few years. The building built on marsh land might well disappear as it was being built. Only the building built on granite could survive as a useful building. Only by spending twice as much money, or even three times as much money in those schools and in those areas of our great cities where the need is greatest, can we possibly give equal opportunities to all school children of those cities.

Tragically enough, the depth of emotion stirred up by racial issues makes it hard for people to see what is best educationally for the children. Elementary schools should be designed as community schools to meet the needs of their particular communities and kept reasonably small, with classroom sizes reduced in proportion to the difficulties to be faced, with special teachers in proportion to the special problems, and with equipment of a variety and richness to serve these teachers to the best advantage and general physical facilities constructed in a creative and imaginative way. Then at the junior high and senior high levels students could select those schools which offered them the education their talents required. Segregation at the junior high and senior high levels would be greatly reduced, for talent, ability and creativity are no respecters of "color curtains" or "racial curtains" or "economic curtains."

At the secondary level children can be bussed considerable distances without any appreciable harm to them or to their education. The community aspect of a school, so very important at the elementary level where the families must be involved in the day-by-day schooling of their children, has less importance at the secondary level. Great cities could easily organize their high schools, for instance, so that the first two years, freshman and sophomore, were devoted to what might be called general education, and the last two years to more specialized education.

Beyond a certain level of academic achievement it is desirable to have social integration, but it is not sensible to strive for total academic integration. Not everyone wishes to be a physicist, not everyone wishes to major in English, not everyone wishes to carry on the study of a foreign language indefinitely. If these choices were available at the secondary levels as has been said, racial and other kinds of harmful segregation would be lessened. But to achieve these kinds of desirable goals at the secondary level, quality education must take place at the elementary level. In this brief glimpse, therefore, of what now exists and what we can expect in the future, the kind of training required by an elementary teacher becomes quite apparent.

As the principal of an elementary school, I would not be distressed if a third grade student could explain more clearly than his own third grade teacher how it was possible for Colonel John Glenn to orbit the earth. But I would, as the principal of this school, be greatly upset if that same third grade student came to class full of excitement about his experience in reading *The Wind in the Willows* or *Alice in Wonderland* and then discovered that the teacher had never read these books. It is a fact that there are many teachers who have not read the books which would most benefit, stimulate, and excite their students. There are many teachers who, because of their lack of training and education, teach as though each one of their children was reading at the same level of ability, and was interested in the same type of book. Often new teachers will proudly say, when interviewed for a position, that they plan to have three reading levels in their classroom. Granted that it is better to have three than one reading level, but if there are twenty-five children in that classroom the teacher had better plan to have twenty-five reading levels! That is, the teacher should know enough to be able to provide twenty-five different levels of enriching reading materials for her children.

An older teacher told this story on herself to illustrate

the need for "a level for each child." In the front lobby of the Laboratory Schools of the University of Chicago there is a massive fireplace on the south wall with a bust of the first principal, Colonel Francis W. Parker, and an inscription from his writing: TRUE EDUCATION FREES THE HUMAN SPIRIT. Opposite, across the lobby, are some cushioned stone benches.

Johnny, a kindergartener, had been rebelling in class because the teacher wanted all the class to take part in rhythm exercises. Johnny wanted to read. Finally, Johnny became such a nuisance that the teacher sent him out of class to sit on one of the benches in the lobby. After a while she came out to see how Johnny was. He greeted her with a big smile and, pointing to the inscription on the fireplace, cried out happily, "You see I want to read so that I can get a true education that will free me from silly rhythms!"

The teaching of skills in reading can well be conducted in larger groups, but the teaching of reading for understanding and for inspiration must be an individual matter. The child, in any given classroom, will be limited by only one factor — the depth and height of the teacher's own richness and background. If she is a "three-level reader" in her own life, then the class will be a three-level class. If she is a "five-hundred-level reader" in her own life, then no matter what end of the spectrum of ability the individual child occupies he will benefit from her teaching.

If you are truly interested in becoming an elementary teacher, start immediately to read books that librarians,

teachers, and organizations believe are worthwile for elementary school children. A number of fine lists are prepared by the American Library Association, the Elementary Teachers Association, and the National Association of
Independent Schools. Your school and city librarians will
have other lists that will be useful to you. Elementary
teachers in your neighborhood, particularly the experienced ones, will have lists. Good bookstores will have dis-
plays of new books. Browse around as much as possible in
libraries and bookstores.

Recently a very good school district which prided itself
on the quality of its education made a survey of its six elementary schools to find out whether a minimum list of
"classics" were available in each of these schools for the
children to read. This list was an arbitrary list prepared by
the librarians and a committee of elementary teachers of
that district, but it was a list that in general would not be
disputed by any experienced person. A few titles might be
added, a few might even be crossed out, but the bulk of the
list could be agreed upon by almost any thoughtful teacher.
To the horror of the superintendent of this school district
it was discovered that no one school of the six had the full
list and that some of the schools had only a tenth of the
titles listed as classics. The children of this wealthy district
were being deprived of their rightful heritage. There are
books which every child should have an opportunity to
read. These are the recognized classics. No school child
should be denied the opportunity of having attractive,
fresh copies of these books. Many good books are being

published every year and these also should be read, although they do not take the place of the classics.

Obviously, if a teacher is not aware of the great books that have stood the test of time, then there is very little chance that the children in her class will ever hear of them. It is not just enough for the teacher to know the titles; the books must have been read by her. Then she will be able to put a particular book in the hands of an individual child when he is ready for it. Every classic will not necessarily be right for every child. Furthermore, the timing of when a child receives a book is of the utmost importance. *Alice in Wonderland,* for instance, might seem like a sissy book to a little boy at a given stage of his development, whereas *The Wind in the Willows* might seem to a little girl at a certain stage of her development as a book about a nasty rat! A year or two before for the boy or after for the girl might be exactly right.

The necessity of reading on one's own emphasizes the fact that formal training received in a college or university is never enough. A person who plans to be a teacher should begin at the earliest possible moment to train himself. Freshmen in high school who are thinking about teaching should begin to prepare themselves. There are even organizations, Future Teachers of America, for instance, which promote a greater understanding of teaching at the high school level by giving students something significant to do. But even membership in this excellent group is not enough. Basically, the kind of training that has been described must be acquired on your own. Any book is worth reading even if it is used only once with one child in a lifetime of teaching. Certain books are also worth reading although you will never use them because you will discover that they would be a waste of the child's time. So as you look towards training yourself as a teacher, begin by reading, and never stop. Read, read, and read!

In almost every community there are opportunities to work with children — as a baby-sitter, as a playground assistant, as a camp counselor, and more recently as a tutor. Take advantage of as many of these opportunities as you can. You will learn something from each experience. Resist the temptation to go back and do the same thing summer after summer or time after time. Keep trying new experiences with different kinds of children. Each time you have such an opportunity it will broaden you and make you a better person and, therefore, a better teacher. You may be a good swimmer or a good rider or a good dancer. Teaching any one of these skills can be just as revealing, just as beneficial to you as teaching reading or arithmetic at this early stage of your development.

Teaching involves two major factors: knowledge — you must know as much as possible about what you are to teach; and methods of teaching — you must understand how children learn and be able to present your knowledge in a way as to benefit the child. And note that the benefit is to *the* child. You will never succeed in teaching children, if that means a group. Always think and work toward teaching the child, the individual. Both factors are essential, knowledge and method. Knowledge without method can be frustrating to the teacher and damaging to the child; method without knowledge can destroy the integrity of the teacher and produce a superficial learner who has been given no resources, no richness. It is as though the child were being fed only on vitamin pills that kept him alive but wasted away his body and soul in the process.

In any college or university the road to knowledge will be pointed out. It will be up to the student to march along that road taking in as much as he can along the way and continuing down that road for the rest of his life. No college can give you all the knowledge you need, but it can point the way, it can make suggestions, it can raise questions about which road to take at a crossroads and which hills to climb. Methods have to be learned from experts. Methods then must be practiced, and gradually the creativity, imagination and skill of the teacher will adapt the methods learned to the particular genius of that teacher and to the needs of the individual children in the classroom. But first must come knowledge, for methods are worthless and hollow gestures without an inexhaustible reservoir of knowledge to give them life.

Without any question the best training available today for the person who wishes to go into elementary education is a four-year liberal arts curriculum given by imaginative and exciting teachers. Hundreds of liberal arts colleges for men or women offer such a curriculum; so do a great number of co-educational colleges and great universities, both private and state. To a lesser degree, but happily, in an increasing number of teachers colleges a broad fundamental education is being offered. More and more superintendents and principals of schools are looking favorably on candidates for elementary positions who have majored in some area of the humanities and minored in education, rather than the reverse. Concentrate heavily on the humanities as an undergraduate and take education courses to fulfill the required minimum. Congressman William S. Moorhead said in his address "For the Establishment of a National Foundation for the Humanities," delivered before the Deans of the Graduate Schools of The Association of State Universities and Land-Grant Colleges, November 9, 1964:

> The educated man recognizes that the humanities are the study of that which is most human. They record not only our lives but the very substance of which our lives are made. The humanities speak for our beliefs, our ideals and our highest achievements.

Later on, graduate level education courses can be stimulating and rewarding. They should be taken with a background of experience in the classroom for then they will have a meaning and value not apparent to the undergraduate who has not yet had the actual experience of teaching. Besides literature courses and basic mathematics courses, the greatest benefit to the undergraduate who plans to go into elementary teaching will come from history, anthropology, archaeology, political science, and art and music courses. If possible, psychology courses should also be taken at the undergraduate level, both for their own value and as preparation for better understanding of the higher level psychology courses that will be taken in graduate school in the field of education. Increasingly, today, some understanding of statistics and tests and measurement is important for all teachers. Naïveté in the area of tests can be disastrous to a teacher and to his students.

If economically possible, a five-year-course plan is desirable for the training of an elementary teacher. In the appendices of this book are lists of colleges and universities which offer the MAT (Master of Arts in Teaching) program for elementary teachers. This is a program by which the teacher candidate completes a four-year liberal arts course and then by an added year gains a Master's Degree in teaching together with an adequate practice-teaching experience. Such a scheme is, of course, economically demanding, and for many too demanding.

The emphasis should always be upon self-training to complement formal training or to compensate for its inadequacies. Take the girl who lives in a rural area with a local teachers college. She can do a great deal on her own to enrich her experience. The local college will offer a basic training. Individual professors in that college, if approached, can be of tremendous help in advising and guiding the undergraduate student. Summer opportunities abound, particularly in big cities. A person who has lived in a rural area and who is going to the local college should make every effort to get a summer job in a big city — on a playground, in a library, or as an assistant in some specialized school. The contrast of the city population with its many cultural backgrounds will be striking to the person brought up in a rural area. The experience of such an "exposure" will be broadening and valuable.

Have the long view about your training as an elementary teacher. If you are a woman and expect to get married after a few years, remember that more and more married women return to teaching after their children reach school age. In fact, these women have become one of the strongest elements in our educational system. There is a shortage of newly trained teachers throughout the United States and this shortage will continue into the observable future. The shortage would be disastrous if it were not for the mature, experienced mothers who have come back into teaching. However, if they have not been properly trained originally, their added maturity as mothers of families will not compensate adequately for their professional shortcomings.

Besides the academic training that must be considered a minimum for anyone and for which only a brief guideline has so far been given, there are other areas that elementary teachers should consider. For instance, the ability to sing and to play a piano, although not essential to an elementary teacher, are of great value. In fact, the playing of any instrument can be a great asset. Not everyone possesses a good singing voice, but there are very few people who can't do some singing and who would not be capable of leading their class in song. Even though the school in which you teach has a music specialist, the ability to create music yourself in your own classroom can be very important. There will be times in every day when you sense that a change of tempo, a change of mood is needed in the class, and nothing is more successful than to engage the children in some form of musical activity.

The ability to teach the creative and applied arts is important. Most teacher-training courses are inadequate in the preparation of elementary teachers in this area. Practical arts courses as well as art appreciation courses should be taken by students, if necessary during the summers between their academic courses. Again, some schools have art specialists, but they can spend only a limited time in any one classroom. Art can be usefully taught as an integral part of every subject in the curriculum. Understanding and appreciation of art should be present in your classroom at all times for the benefit of the child. Art can be found in the style of the desk, the architecture of the school building, in the changing color of the leaves on the tree outside the window, as well as in the reproductions which you have placed on the walls of your room. Visits to art museums can be among the most rewarding and exciting experiences of the year for the children. The teacher must prepare for these visits and then follow up after each visit to accomplish a true learning experience.

It is not enough that the teacher or the guide at the museum do an excellent job while going through the gallery. Art must be a part of the daily life of the classroom so that the visit to the museum becomes an extension of the class activity and not an isolated event. Knowledge of museums, for instance, and of the great works of art to be found in them, will not be learned in a formal setting. To prepare yourself as a teacher, take time to visit art museums, read books on art, and decide for yourself what you would like to introduce to the children in the classes you will have.

There are many schools which still require their elementary teachers to carry on whatever physical education is offered to the children. Happily, the number of schools in this category is gradually being reduced every year. But even if there is a physical education specialist, it is well for an elementary teacher to understand the philosophy of the physical education program. As you study science, social studies, or art and music, you will find opportunities to support this basic philosophy of physical education. For a true physical education program involves not only an understanding of anatomy, physiology, and the major muscular functions. It also involves an understanding of hygiene, diet, and rhythm. Anyone who watched the Olympic Games performers saw in the gymnast, for instance, rhythm of a musical nature with postures that were classic in their art form, employing muscular skill and control that would appear unbelievable without a knowledge of the fabulous potentials of our body structure.

Finally, even though a school may have a physical education specialist, most elementary teachers are required to have recess and playtime duty. Sometimes a completely free playtime is desirable. Other times, in particular situations, the suggestion of a game can mean a successful day for all the children instead of a demoralizing and unhappy one. It is good for children to learn to play on their own, but not always. It is good for children to have organized games, but not always. Sometimes, because of bad weather and the physical facilities of the school, it is necessary to have the playtime in very crowded indoor quarters when free play would be disastrous. To know one or two games is not enough, any more than to know one or two books is enough. Games have their roots in the earliest civilizations. Games are based on fundamental emotions. The right game chosen at the right time can be as instructive and as beneficial as any experience a child will have during the course of a school day. The child who is having trouble in reading may find satisfaction during recess time and regain the self-respect he was losing in the classroom.

To extend your knowledge beyond the academic and specialized training, start reading professional journals. The *NEA Journal,* for instance, is of a general nature and many of its articles are directed towards the interests of elementary teachers. The *Elementary School Journal,* published at the University of Chicago, has stimulating articles in every issue for elementary teachers. Almost all newspapers have sections on education today. The *New York Sunday Times,* for instance, devotes a page to education and much of it has to do with elementary education.

It is well to consider the broader issues of education as you see them locally, nationally, and internationally. State offices of education, the Federal Office of Education, and the United Nations Office of Education all issue regular publications and pamphlets which deal with questions of interest to you. These can be acquired by simply asking for them. The elementary classroom is the barometer of social conditions. Within this classroom will be reflected in microcosm the conditions that exist in the world immediately outside and in the world in general. The elementary classroom teacher who is sensitive to the needs and concerns of her children may well sense changes earlier than the trained political scientist.

It is important, therefore, that the elementary teacher keep as alert as possible to world developments and to local developments if he or she is to do the best possible job for each child. The understanding of each child, an essential for an elementary teacher, which is gained by personal knowledge of the child, and the information received from the guidance counselor and the principal is still not enough to help the child to the utmost. The teacher also must know something about the condition of the community from which the child comes and the forces, local, national, and international, which are affecting the child, his family, and his community.

A knowledge of baseball, the ability to identify a pileated woodpecker, the love of madrigals, a knowledge of the Stock Exchange, an appreciation of the sculpture of Rodin and of Henry Moore, the daily concerns of retailing, an understanding of military ranks — any one of these accomplishments may at any given moment with any given child be the source of an illustration that will help the child learn. Although all of us would be proud to be compared to Lincoln, let us hope no teacher, looking back, need feel as he did about his education. In filling out an autobiographical sketch for the *Congressional Record* when he was a Congressman he noted after the section marked education: Defective!

2 How to Teach Our Heritage

All social movements involve conflicts which are reflected intellectually in controversies. It would not be a sign of health if such an important social interest as education were not also an arena of struggles, practical and theoretical. . . . It is the business of an intelligent theory of education to ascertain the causes for the conflicts that exist and then, instead of taking one side or the other, to indicate a plan of operations proceeding from a level deeper and more inclusive than is represented by the practices and ideas of the contending parties.

— John Dewey, *Experience and Education*

Today more than ever before you hear and read about the failure of education to prepare children for living in their world. The "social movements" of which John Dewey speaks are many, violent, and conflicting. The "causes of conflict" appear to be more complex, more diverse, and more critical than society has ever faced in its history. Economic and political outcomes are becoming increasingly dependent upon the solutions that are reached by the schools. The threat of deterioration of the great "inner cities," the location and expansion of industry, the amount and design of housing, and racial and civil rights issues are having a direct influence on how schools are organized, what the curriculum should be, and *how and in what manner teachers should be trained*.

The experience of Don Grant, a teacher in one of our big cities, illustrates how the pressures from all the elements listed above can focus on an individual teacher. Don Grant was a man who, from all the evidence available, had been a success for better than twenty years as a homeroom teacher of a sixth grade class in an elementary school of a big city. He had completed his formal training for his degree and certification requirements in the forties, and after military service in the war returned to teaching. From time to time he took summer courses in his fields of interest. His classes over the years had averaged twenty-five in the number of pupils enrolled. The children represented a lower-middle to middle-class economic background, they were well "integrated," that is to say that ethnically, racially, and religiously there was a reasonable balance. Chronologically, there was a two- to three-year age span. Measured by IQ there was a range of 90 to 120, and by reading ability for this sixth grade class a range from fourth grade through eighth grade. This particular pattern of class composition was as typical of the average big city class as one could find at the time Don Grant started to teach. The conditions on the whole were good. It wasn't the "best," if by that is meant high average IQ and homogeneity, nor was it the "worst," if by that is meant low average IQ and a background of impoverishment.

Most of the teachers in Don's school had been there for many years and as a consequence there was good morale in the staff. And finally, and this is a factor of extreme importance, Don Grant expected at least twenty of the twenty-five students who were enrolled at the opening of the school in September to be present when school ended in June.

The special service teachers in physical education, in speech therapy, in library services, in psychological testing, in music, and in art were available at scheduled times, some daily, some weekly, and some on special call. The books and materials prescribed were appropriate for the education of the children and were easily obtainable in sufficient quantity. The school building and surrounding play yard were old but well maintained and not overcrowded, and vandalism was a minor factor in upkeep.

In the city as a whole there was confidence in the school board and in the administration of the schools. Tax levies and bond issues were passed without controversy. There was no illusion that this was the best possible school district or that the school authorities provided the best possible education for the children in their charge. However, shortcomings were identifiable, plans were being developed regularly by the central office research staff and, typically, improvements and changes were anticipated as part of the on-going nature of the school program.

In the world at the conclusion of World War II, there was general optimism. Only one nation, the United States, possessed the bomb. In the eyes of our Western allies who favored some form of democratic political existence, our country appeared benign and anxious to help rather than hinder their rehabilitation. The true implications of the nuclear age, automation, cybernetics (where control of work, as well as the work itself, is taken over by machines), the "emerging nations," world population explosions, and the high mobility of peoples, expressed locally by the migration of rural inhabitants to urban centers, were not generally understood. In fact they were not even being discussed in the daily press or in popular magazines. A few thoughtful scholars were writing for professional journals about developments and consequences which they foresaw and which they feared. But their ideas were thought to be the products of impractical ivory tower dwellers or the cries of radicals!

The training of teachers before the war and also immediately after the war was of a traditional nature that had not changed in substance, despite changes in particulars, during the preceding forty years. Certainly the training of the majority of teachers, which took place in teachers colleges and state universities, did not anticipate or reflect the conditions which the world, the United States, our big cities, and specifically Don Grant, face now and will have to face for some time to come.

What happened? Let us begin again with Don Grant in the sixth grade homeroom in an elementary school of one of our big-city public school systems. Within a very short period of time, with surprisingly little warning, the following violent changes took place that had an immediate influence on the teaching effectiveness of Don Grant.

The average size of his class rose from twenty-five to thirty-five. Economically the children now represented, by census definition, the poor. They were totally segregated as to race, all being Negroes. Religious backgrounds were now limited to Catholic for the Puerto Ricans and Pentecostal Protestant sects for the others. Chronologically the age span had increased from two to three years to a difference of six years. In IQ measurement the differences were narrowed from a range of 90 to 120 to a grouping around 80 to 90 with a very occasional individual child at 100. In this sixth grade class the *average* level of reading ability was third grade and the range was from illiterate to a high of fifth grade. Within a year two-thirds of the experienced senior teachers had been transferred to other schools and had been replaced by first year teachers or by uncertified "permanent substitute" teachers.

At the end of the year only five students of the original thirty-five or forty children who had enrolled in September were still enrolled. The special service teachers, particularly those assigned to the building in physical education, in music and in art, were almost never available for scheduled classes in their specialties, since they were constantly being asked to substitute for homeroom teachers who were absent. The "traveling" service teachers in speech therapy, testing, psychological counseling and tutoring had decreased in total numbers. Those that remained had, because of the growth in numbers of children, a load that had doubled or tripled in size. The obvious result was that Don Grant, the homeroom teacher, had little hope that more than a small portion of his children who needed this service would ever get it. Discipline problems within the school were on the increase and required more of the energy, emotional commitment and time of the teacher.

The books provided for the sixth grade were now inappropriate, and because of the sudden increase in numbers of students city-wide at the elementary level, materials were in short supply and slow to be delivered. In an attempt to get books that were more suited to the reading level of the class, Grant first tried through "channels" to get third grade readers for his sixth grade. When that proved impossible he was able, by talking to friends in other schools, to assemble a set. Unfortunately, the series used by this city school system had the number of the grade level imprinted on the cover of each book. The class, when they saw the number "3," protested vehemently and declared they were sixth graders and would not work with third grade books.

The school building, which had been built around 1910, had been designed to hold 50 per cent fewer students than now crowded every classroom, the lavatory facilities, the halls and the playground. It was no longer possible to maintain the building properly, and the physical condition became daily worse. Vandalism during after-school hours and over the weekends became an increasingly serious problem and accelerated the deterioration of the building and the play yard.

Numbers. Sheer numbers of persons forced to live in small areas. Twice as many children forced to go to school in a building built for half their number. What can almost be called "jungle law," a survival of the fittest, takes over when conditions get too crowded. A new code of conduct emerged that had little resemblance to established law and order, as Don Grant discovered. One day he bought a brand-new "Chevy," the first new car he had ever owned, and drove it to school, parking in his accustomed place. When he came out after school to drive home all four hubcaps and the outside rear-view mirror had been removed. He stood bewildered, too shocked even to be angry, looking at his cannibalized car. One of the big, over-age boys from his class came up to him.

"Mr. Grant, is that your car?"

"Why, yes, John. What's left of it."

"Mr. Grant, we thought you drove an old '55 Ford."

"I did, John, but I bought this yesterday."

"Oh my, Mr. Grant. We didn't know that. Mr. Grant, I suspect you need to go see Mr. Maloney [the principal]."

"Why's that, John?"

"Yes, you go see the principal, Mr. Grant."

Don Grant sensed something was up and went off to the principal's office. When he returned the rear-view mirror and all the hubcaps were in place. Apparently the boys had thought this new car belonged to a salesman, a stranger, who was fair game.

The conflicting pressures on the mayor's office and on the board of education mounted as social conditions became critical and the inadequacies of the education being offered the children became apparent. The staff of the central office of the city schools, highly competent professionals, could no longer spend sufficient time to analyze rapidly changing conditions or to plan how to meet the needs of the children now in the schools. Those at the administration level most able to carry out research and to experiment and innovate were called upon to put out one local "brush fire" after another. The public began to have serious doubts about the effectiveness of the board of education. Beset by economic and social worries brought on by the "flight" to the suburbs of many substantial white residents, by threatened land devaluation, and by loss of major industries, the voters defeated desperately needed school tax levies and bond issues. Denied the money necessary to meet the changing conditions, the school board found itself daily in a more serious condition. Don Grant and his students became the unwilling victims of these new forces.

World conditions in the sixties no longer produced unqualified optimism. At least five nations possessed nuclear weapons. Every working man, white and blue collar alike, was influenced by automation and increasingly by developments in cybernetics. The nations of Africa and South America emerged as full voting members of the United Nations, thereby doubling the size of the membership since 1945. The increased size of this great world organization naturally added to the tensions and produced divisions among the member states that made consensus more difficult to come by. Growth of world population was a recognized threat to world health and peace. The migration of peoples within the United States shifted the majority of our population from rural to urban centers with a speed and to an extent that indicated that by 1975 three-quarters of our citizens would live in the big cities. All these factors and many more determine what Don Grant can do for his school children.

How did it happen? Why has the speed of change accelerated to such a degree? There is no one that can give us all the answers, since it is questionable that all the factors are known or understood. To discuss the question adequately would require a book in itself. Our purpose is to indicate a few of the major factors and to emphasize that their inevitability was certain and beyond control.

Man's insatiable quest for knowledge, which drove Copernicus, Galileo, Newton, and finally Einstein to their revolutionary findings, is the basic cause. The factor of speed is related to the new knowledge and understanding of our world, since inventions of a practical nature follow the development of theory. Communication and travel between peoples has taken full advantage of new inventions, just as controlled power has been harnessed in ways that portend great good for mankind or threaten total destruction. Remember that the jump from the Pony Express to the transcontinental railroad was no less revolutionary than the jump from the railroad to the jet plane, or from the jet plane to the space capsule!

Because of the increased power to communicate by radio and television (direct world-wide visual coverage by Early Bird Satellite in your own living room), human rights all over the world have been exposed for all to understand. As the old spiritual said many years ago, "there is no North, there is no South, there is no East, there is no West" any longer in our world. Human conscience as well as human inventiveness has been stirred in new and powerful ways. Learning about, organizing in an orderly fashion, and finally understanding the new knowledge is what is necessary for each person to do. Teachers in the schools have to accept this responsibility in the education of youth. The kind of training a teacher receives is, as it always has been, vital to the whole enterprise.

Is it hopeless to think of educating adequately the children already born? Should we devote ourselves only to preparing for the future? The present conditions are indeed serious, but they are not hopeless. The degree of seriousness varies from schools in our big cities to the schools in remote rural areas, but the basic inadequacies for each type of school remain similar and critical. With the increased mobility of our peoples and the exposure to nationwide radio and television the need for urban and rural education differences will be unimportant. The necessity for the city boy and the farm boy to read and to understand what they read is of equal importance. The need to grasp world affairs is shared by all. Racial and religious differences must be understood by all for what they are and not be obscured by prejudices, superstitions and myths. Finally, our democratic form of life must face up to the poverty, the deprivations, the bigotry that exist in our country as well as to the glories of our freedom, our laws and our institutions.

Recognizing the immediacy of the needs, the Federal Government in 1965 enacted the Anti-Poverty Act and the Primary and Secondary School Acts. These were milestones of tremendous importance in an all-out attack on the problems that faced Don Grant, sixth grade teacher. Continuing in importance are the opportunities offered teachers to better prepare themselves for present conditions, such as the fellowships for further study awarded by the National Science Foundation (NSF) and by the National Defense Education Act (NDEA). Besides these massive Federal programs are countless state- and city-supported projects and countless training and research opportunities offered by private foundations, such as Ford, Rockefeller, Carnegie, and Danforth, to mention only a few of the largest.

You could not select a more exciting, a more vital, a more important period of time in which to become involved as a teacher than the present. We must believe for our students and for ourselves what John Dewey said in *Experience and Education,* "The most important attitude that can be formed is that of desire to go on learning" so that our common heritage can be taught by Don Grant and by you to all the children in our country's schools.

3   The Different Levels of Teaching

THERE are a number of distinct levels of teaching in elementary schools. The level at which you teach, just as the type of school district and the character of the community which you choose, is a personal matter. You must know yourself so that you can judge at what level your interests and competence will best satisfy your needs and best serve the children you teach.

The levels can be divided as follows: (1) Nursery school, where children are between three and four years old on entrance; (2) Kindergarten, traditionally five years of age on entrance but many variations in school admittance regulations actually produce at least an eighteen-month span, sometimes a two-year span; (3) Grade 1, where for the majority learning to read will begin; (4) Grades 2, 3, and 4, where enrichment and development of skills in reading, writing, speech, and concept of numbers takes place in varying degrees; (5) Grades 5 and 6, where the limits in most school districts of the "self-contained" classroom are reached, and where many specialists are called upon to assist; and finally (6) Grades 7 and 8, which in some school districts are still considered part of the elementary school, but which increasingly are part of a junior high school or middle school arrangement. Given the basic qualifications, the demands on the teacher are very different at almost each level.

NURSERY SCHOOL

So far in the United States, there are no public school systems which offer all children an opportunity to attend nursery schools supported by tax monies. Public money, mostly Federal or state rather than local, is beginning to be spent in a few pilot or experimental situations in the big cities. It is of interest that Russia, which because of its increased industrialization faces a phenomenal growth of its big cities, has instituted state-operated nursery schools beginning with one-year-olds which extend for the whole day. With both parents working, the Russian government realized that it had to do something to provide for the children. From all reports, the day nursery schools operating in Moscow, Leningrad, and Kiev are good by pedagogical and psychological worldwide standards.

Since public school districts do not have nursery schools, they have been organized by private groups, some incorporated and nonprofit, some operated as part of church programs, some by settlement houses or other organizations serving youth, and some proprietary for profit. In general, proprietary schools, that is schools owned and operated by an individual or a family, are hampered financially in ways that seriously restrict the program they can offer. There are, of course, some exceptions to this general condition. Some nursery schools are little more than organized group baby-sitting. In schools of this type there is no attempt to accomplish particular goals through a planned program.

Nursery schools in the United States are concentrated primarily in big cities, and in the suburbs of those cities, although in an increasing number of small towns nursery schools are being formed. Some of these schools are operated on the principles developed by Madame Montessori, described on page 47. This increasing interest in nursery school education is demonstrated by the amount of time, money, and top-flight personnel which institutions of the caliber of the University of Chicago (the Laboratory Schools), Tufts University (the Eliot Pearson School), and Wayne State University of Detroit (the Merrill-Palmer School) are devoting to the training of nursery school teachers.

Why has the training of nursery school teachers become increasingly important in the United States? This importance has grown because of two almost diametrically opposed demands. The first need arose as it became evident that children could be trained earlier. The other reason for the increased interest in nursery school education and for trained teachers at this level has been the important and critical situation developing in the great cities of our country as more and more people from rural areas migrate to urban centers. Many of the Negro and white immigrants from the deep South and Appalachian mountain areas, for instance, have come to the city with little or no tradition of schooling, and almost no idea of how to live in a community of people as closely packed together as they are in a city.

In the first instance, with so much new knowledge there was not enough time in the traditional span of school and college to educate people for the professions, particularly in the sciences. The lack of knowledge and of skills which the professional schools complained of resulted in a chain reaction. The graduate universities asked the colleges to do more, who in turn asked the secondary schools for more advanced work. The secondary schools thus found themselves teaching at levels reserved for colleges only a few years ago.

It was obvious the most basic change would have to take

place in the elementary grades. And so the nursery school, reflecting the turmoil above it, began to think in a systematic and philosophic way about the education of its children. Much of the "social adjustment" that took place in kindergarten and first grade could be accomplished as well in nursery school.

Nursery schools in urban areas, amongst culturally deprived groups, became important because children who enrolled at the first grade level were found to lack a knowledge of social conditions and relationships, and of cultural standards required of those living in big cities. They were not prepared to begin to learn to read or to deal with numbers and logical relationships. By the third grade, if they had no pre-school training, many were already one to three years behind their contemporaries who had come from more advantaged social and economic backgrounds.

Along with the practical needs for earlier education, it has become apparent to educators that three-years-olds and four-year-olds as well as the traditional five-year-olds of kindergarten can gain much from well-organized schools. At this age of learning, subject matter content is almost nonexistent. Verbalization and concept forming is in its early and primitive stages. Teaching in its traditional meaning of transmitting knowledge is not what is called for. Therefore, the characteristics that make for successful nursery school and kindergarten teachers are special in many respects, even though they include many traits that are true of all good teachers at whatever level they may teach.

In listing those characteristics and aptitudes which good

nursery school teachers possess, great emphasis is placed upon relations with the child at a personal level, with willingness to deal with the parents of the child, and with the ability to observe rather than to direct, to guide rather than to lead. Many people who are highly successful and exciting teachers of subject matter at the fifth or sixth grade level would be impatient, frustrated, and even irritated by dealing with children of three or four years of age. To state this fact is merely to emphasize the different personalities required at different levels. At all levels there are great teachers. There is no way of saying which is the finest, but that they are different is true, and important for anyone to know who is considering teaching as a profession.

In general the nursery school teacher should like and respect young children and enjoy working with them and their parents on warm and friendly terms. Above all, she must be calm, sensitive, and thoughtful of others, and have a genuine sense of humor. She should be able to understand how young children grow, think, behave and learn. Besides, she must have a strong belief in the value of each phase of a child's growth so that she can recognize where he is in his development and be sensitive to the growth and learning needs of the individual child. Through understandings of this kind, the teacher can help the child move forward at the child's own rate of development.

Yet even these understandings are not sufficient for the teacher of nursery school children. There must also be clear understanding and appreciation of how children develop independence, resourcefulness, creativity, a sense of responsibility, and the ability to solve problems.

Basically, much of the child's growth and development will take place naturally if the teacher is an expert observer, able by watching and listening to gather clues to the needs of her pupils. This habit of observation should dominate her entire approach to teaching. If she is successful, she will be able to support and extend the child's effort, answering questions and guiding play so that it challenges his capacities as he becomes ready for different kinds of experience. Furthermore, she will be flexible enough to change plans and programs according to the needs of the individual child and the group. By trained observation of this nature, the teacher will recognize children who are excessively shy and timid, those who are aggressive and belligerent, those whose nutrition is poor, those who have serious defects, and those whose cultural background is limited or different. The teacher will also be trained to know when to seek professional assistance and when to refer to experts in various areas.

Never assume that nursery school age children are not sensitive and understanding. In fact they may sometimes even express themselves in a manner thought to be reserved for adults. Recently at the University of Chicago a well-known professor only forty-two years old died after a long illness. He had married late in life and had one three-and-a-half-year-old son. One of the early games played by the mother with her son was to say, "You are my sweetheart," and the little boy would answer, "No, I'm your boy." A few days after her husband's death she said to her son, "You are my boy." "No," the little boy answered, "now I am your man."

What exactly goes on in a nursery school? How is the program original? What goals are sought after? And what are some of the methods of instruction? In a talk before the Guidance and Counseling Department of the Laboratory Schools of the University of Chicago, Dr. William Fowler, then Principal of the Nursery School and Assistant Professor at the Graduate School of Education of the University of Chicago, gave some of the answers to these questions. Dr. Fowler's philosophy represents the best thinking of scholars in this area of education. His position can be summarized under five headings:

1) THEORETICAL FRAMEWORK: Characterized as a "human development" approach, based on an analysis of the life of the classroom and available information about the students and their families.

2) AMOUNT OF TIME SPENT IN STIMULATING LOGICAL THINKING: In principle, this stimulation cannot really be isolated from the total nursery program. However, each child participates in two or three relatively structured projects in reading, mathematics, or science. Project periods are interspersed with free play, juice, etc. The frequency during a week varies according to the subject area: e.g., reading is taught every day because of the importance of memory in developing reading skills. Since rates of learning

differ, children within a single group may be engaged in different activities, but there is enough common activity to preserve the group identity.

3) METHODS OF INSTRUCTION: Emphasis is on plays and games; e.g., in the reading program a child may use word or picture cards in target games, or search-and-find games. In some instances the teacher may narrate a story and the children role-play. Many of the games are basically discrimination-sorting tasks, in which classifications are developed; e.g., in science the children place animals in their proper habitat or in a painted ecological background.

4) FORMATION OF GROUPS: Classes are composed to have balanced representations of age and sex. Ideally, each child can have the experience of being at different ends of the age span in his first and second years, and thus be able to assume both leader and follower roles. Small project groups are also composed with an eye to variety in development and with regard to ability in the area being taught.

5) SEX DIFFERENCES: In general, the girls are found to be more adept at interpersonal relations, and the boys more adept in the world of "things," because of the play situations provided prior to nursery school entrance. An attempt is made to supply experiences that will equalize these competencies.

The Montessori schools have been mentioned before. What was their origin? Maria Montessori, a member of an old and distinguished Italian family, trained herself as a psychiatrist in Rome. At the turn of the century she began to develop a system of training children at an early age in what were known as infant schools designed particularly for the working-class people of Rome. She incorporated into her system much of the best knowledge of the day and based her techniques on accepted psychological practices and educational theories developed by Rousseau, Froebel, and Pestalozzi. She also used techniques that had been developed by various experts in the training of mentally retarded children.

The reasonableness of Madame Montessori's approach led persons in many lands to adopt her methods, and for many years before the First World War there were a growing number of schools in the United States. For various reasons, not significant for this book, there was a lessening of interest between the two World Wars. Recently, however, there has been a new birth of Montessori schools in the United States. One thing which has re-created this interest is the concern of many people that educators have been ignoring the three r's — reading, writing, and arithmetic. Concerns of this nature also led to the establishment of the Council for Basic Education. In any event, Montessori schools and Montessori methods are now very much in the limelight. Though one may not wish to accept the full Montessori method, one can learn a great deal from the materials that have been developed by these schools and from the techniques employed in their use. To make a simple distinction between the Montessori nursery school and the more traditional nursery school, one might say that the Montessori schools attempt to develop the child's learning capacity by a sequence of rational, organized steps of increasing difficulty; that is, by a "structured" program. In contrast, the traditional method offers free, creative, "unstructured" expression.

Not everyone, as has been emphasized, has the temperament to teach at the nursery school level any more than everyone has the temperament, interest, or competence for any given grade level. It is recommended strongly that visits be made to nursery schools, both conventional and of the Montessori type, to observe what is demanded of teachers, what are the goals of this level of education, and what seem to be the satisfactions of those who work at this level.

KINDERGARTEN

St. Louis was the site of the first public school kindergarten. On December 9, 1873, Superintendent William T. Harris announced the opening of the first school, Des Pères, with Miss Susan Blow as "Director" and Mary A. Timbulake as the first kindergartener! Before Superintendent Harris left St. Louis in 1880, he had opened fifty-five such schools. Harris was influenced greatly by the writing of Froebel (1782-1852), the great German educator and founder of the kindergarten in 1837 at Brandenburg. Privately operated kindergartens had been in existence since 1856 in the United States, when Mrs. Carl Schurz established a school in Watertown, Wisconsin.

According to Kurt Leiderken in *Yankee Teacher*, William Harris and Miss Susan Blow of St. Louis both "advocated instruction in addition to development, and not development *or* knowledge, but development *and* knowledge, and not subjective *or* objective knowledge, but subjective *and* objective knowledge in a harmonious relationship." These ideas followed those of Froebel, who believed in the importance of "self-activity" as the proper road toward learning.

The teacher at this level has a chance to know and to teach what is too often labeled, out of ignorance, the whole child. That is to say the whole nature of the child. In a speech to an assembly of Infant Teachers in England, John Blackie, Chief Inspector of Primary Schools, said "Let us begin by reminding ourselves that the nature *is* a whole . . . the child remains indivisible . . . his physical, emotional, intellectual and spiritual functions are not separate but are inextricably intertwined strands in a single whole."

By five years of age, the traditional time for kindergarten, the child has taken tremendous steps from his nursery school years. He is even more curious and anxious to learn. He is beginning to have expressed purposes.

Do you recall the two little kindergarten children who at recess had been discussing the future of nuclear power? The class bell rang and one of the five-year-old boys turned to his friend and said, "Well, I suppose we'll have to go back to class and thread some more beads!"

What are the teacher's goals with the whole nature of the child? What particular responsibility does the kindergarten teacher have with her five-year-olds? Professor

Elenora Moore of Wayne State University believes there are "five common life situations that deserve special attention" — social-emotional weaning, development of security, social adjustment to peers, extension of intellectual horizons, and promoting children's health. It is also interesting to note that this same authority urges all prospective kindergarten teachers to get a liberal education with a strong backing of psychology and of the social sciences. It is indeed demanding on the teacher to be a guide in the child's development of human relations, and to protect him so that he can be free to make choices and explore his own being. It is far easier to impose one's own will on a child than to "listen" and allow him to follow his own line of thought, indirect and winding as that line may be. It takes a truly educated person to know when to let the child "go it alone." In fact, the teacher has to know enough to understand from the barest hint that the road is worth exploring.

In a year-end report Rose Bello, an experienced teacher with the Laboratory Schools of the University of Chicago, tells of "listening":

What did I think I accomplished this year? Teaching young children is among the most creative of human experiences. My best teachers have been my children. It's only when I forget to *listen* that I don't perceive; and by missing clues children give out, the day ends up for all of us — an exhaustingly dull one.

I'd like to tell you about a day I did listen and its gratifying results. It started out during one of those inevitable Show and Tell periods. My contribution was some of my favorite Miró prints. I hung them before school. Nothing was said — by me or the group. No one seemed to be aware of them, but at least I enjoyed looking at them. Finally, one day during Show and Tell I mentioned that I was removing the prints and perhaps they might want to hang some of their favorites. Well — what followed — what *they* saw, how *they* looked at Miró — the relationship between his pictures and the geometric shapes we had been exploring all week (up to that moment I had not seen the connection!) not only deepened my appreciation for the artist but guided me in my choice of artists to share with my group for the next few months. I continued with the abstract artists. I discovered that children attach much more emotion to this style than most adults. One of the reasons, I'm sure, is because young children's schematic drawings have something in common with the artist's ability to abstract the essence from a subject. Unwittingly, I introduced them to the abstract *first* instead of the usual representational. No child said, "What is it?" Or thought them strange. We've hung many artists since — many contributed by children — but Miró remained the most popular. Is it because Miró, more than others, talks most directly to children, or was it because they met him first? I'd like to pursue this further next year. But, much more important, parents have told me that they were obliged to make more trips to the Art Institute than they had planned! Children bought prints — and browsed through many art books seeking their favorite artists. Perhaps, for some, this may become a lifelong habit.

To sum up the particular concerns of anyone thinking of being a kindergarten teacher: it is basic that you are dealing with an active, inquiring child who needs help in becoming independent from his family (social-emotional weaning); who needs a realization of what self-confidence and self-assurance truly involves (development of security); who has to learn to acknowledge the rights of others, to share possessions with others, in short, to be tolerant and respectful of others (social adjustment to peers); who should be encouraged not only to ask what but also why, and who, if he comes to class with some rudimentary skills in reading or number comprehension, should be given opportunities to develop these skills (extension of intellectual horizons); and who should, finally, be introduced to games and exercises that promote health and utilize muscular skills, and be taught basic hygiene and physical safety facts (promoting children's health).

It is evident that the successful kindergarten teacher must be extremely flexible in point of view. There is no known formal curriculum structure that will provide for the evolving emotional nature of a child. A kindergarten teacher has goals and aspirations for her children, but there is no timetable of specifics she can follow. Her objectives if applied to swimming would be to make the child aware of water, to give him an understanding of the gifts, the pleasures, and the dangers of water. The skill of learning to swim is a specific which can be measured. Each child will understand water to a varying degree when he comes to class and each will increase his grasp of it at a different rate of comprehension. There is nothing "neat" and definite when dealing with the whole nature of a child!

FIRST GRADE

The teacher of the first grade has the two most important tasks in the child's education from nursery school through the highest graduate levels. To be the first to introduce an individual to formal reading and to an understanding of number relationships is an awesome responsibility. The importance which scholars and professional educators place on these two tasks is reflected in the countless research projects and the infinite number of books that try to help the first grade teacher do her job. The result is that we know more and more, but we still do not know enough!

If there were as much heated argument between doctors as to how an appendix should be removed as there is between the followers of the "phonetics" approach and the devotees of the "recognition" approach to beginning reading, the patient might almost prefer the appendix to burst and let nature take its course! Fortunately most teachers, observing the individual differences between children, use aspects from both these approaches to reading, as well as other methods they believe best suited to each particular child.

This over-simplification of beginning reading and what it means for the teacher does illustrate forcibly the major difference between a first grade teacher and a nursery school and kindergarten teacher. The first grade teacher is responsible for subject matter — reading and mathematics skills. The emphasis has moved from psychological concerns to more intellectual concerns. The academic curriculum gradually assumes more and more importance in contrast to the emotional and physical adjustments of the nursery school and kindergarten classes. But no matter how great the transition or change from level to level, it never is a question of either-or. It is always both!

The nursery school teacher is very much concerned with whether or not little Johnny pulls little Susie's hair, whereas the professor meeting with his advanced seminar can become greatly upset if one of his students appears inept in the preparation of his bibliography. Nevertheless, it hinders the effectiveness of the professor if personality adjustments are required among his students, in the same way that failing to put away toys on their proper shelves slows down the accomplishments of a day in the nursery school.

Every good first grade teacher strives for an individual reading program for each child. In a class of twenty-five the mechanical aspects of learning to read can usually be taught on three levels, but in comprehension and appreciation of what they are reading there will be, whether or not the teacher recognizes the fact, twenty-five levels! Unless the class is hopelessly overcrowded, the teacher can encourage individual reading by acquiring as many books as possible for her classroom and allowing the children to make their own choices, by encouraging the child's use of the school library, the local public library, and by advising parents on the purchase of books for their children.

The paperback book is a relatively new resource for elementary schools. It has particular values for schools that do not have a library of their own. Dr. Robert Newman of Syracuse University organized a paperback bookstore when he was the principal of the Lower School of the Laboratory Schools of the University of Chicago. In a *Saturday Review* article he raised the question:

> What books, if any, will a child buy in an elementary school paperback bookstore — and why? . . . Paperbacks are an easy hit with the young for several reasons, the most obvious being that small attractive volumes seem less awesome than big heavy books. But paperbacks also apparently appeal to the seven-to-ten-year-old's penchant for collecting and trading, and the youngsters enjoy playing the role of client in a tiny bookshop for children.

This particular store was a great success. Four thousand volumes were sold to a student body of 850 in its first year of operation. There were over 800 different titles for sale. A nearby public school in a neighborhood thought to be "disadvantaged" had an equal success with a store they operated on the same model. The point is clear. A child, any child, wants to read. It is up to the teacher to teach him the skill and offer him countless opportunities to practice. It is very difficult to profit from or enjoy swimming if no water is available in which to plunge!

The best way to introduce numbers and their relationships with one another as well as their uses has undergone an exciting "revolution" in recent years. A Belgian, Cuisenaire, began thinking about how he might teach mathematics to elementary children in a way more effective than the customary rote memory method. He believed that if from the very beginning children could understand, could see the relation of one number to another number they would then have the power to manipulate numbers accurately and meaningfully. The reasons for addition, subtraction, multiplication, division, fractions and equations would be clear and real. Numbers would be a part of their life, the way words are a part of life. There would be an intelligible language of mathematics for even the youngest students.

Among other ideas, Cuisenaire developed "rods," or little colored blocks that helped children see number relationships. From these early and practical experiments, a number of outstanding scholars have gone on to develop whole curriculum sequences for the elementary schools. Children who have teachers trained in this "new look at old math" learn to think as mathematicians.

A newly appointed mathematics supervisor working for New York State had his first experience with "new math" in a small country elementary school in the Adirondack Mountains. When he came into the primary class, the teacher was just beginning the arithmetic lesson for the day. Asking permission to conduct the class he asked, "Will somebody please give me a two-digit number?" "Sixty-eight" was offered. He turned around and wrote 86 on the blackboard. There was no comment from the class, so he tried again. "Seventy-four" came from a little girl in the front row. He wrote 47 on the board; still no objection. He began to wonder if the class was unusually dull or whether they had not learned anything. He tried once more. This time a small, pug-nosed, freckle-faced boy called out "thirty-three and, Mister, let's see you turn that around!"

Besides reading and mathematics, the first grade should have units in social studies and in science. Art and music will support and undergird each of the subject fields, as well as stand on their own values as separate subjects. A teacher of first grade can use her own skill in art and music, both to support all the subjects taught, and to provide a glorious personal experience for each child.

All levels of teaching have equal importance in the education of a child. This book emphasizes that at every opportunity. Every level is similar in many of the demands it makes upon teachers. The basic qualities of intelligence, imagination and humor, together with integrity, competence and physical vigor are necessary at whatever level you teach. In stressing the differences that exist for teachers at the different levels, we do not overlook or minimize the similarities but bring to light special characteristics in order to aid the prospective teacher in selecting the level that appears to fit her interests, talents, and temperament. Clearly there are important differences in the demands made on a nursery school teacher in contrast to those made on a first grade teacher.

SECOND, THIRD AND FOURTH GRADES

This somewhat arbitrary arrangement of grades has been selected to consider as a group because of the growing tendency to organize elementary schools K-4. In many public school districts, each grade within this span is maintained as a "self-contained" classroom. Basically, this means that a homeroom teacher is responsible for the major subject matter areas of language arts, social studies, mathematics, science and art. In an equally large number this span has self-contained classrooms in the charge of homeroom teachers with the one exception of physical education. A few will also add a music specialist who takes the class for a period once or twice a week. Physical education and music are also taught by homeroom teachers in many schools.

Throughout the second, third, and fourth grades the greatest emphasis must be placed on reading and number relationships. As in a foot race, the longer the race, the greater the distance separating the front runner from the one bringing up the rear. So it is with the basic skills of children in a typically non-grouped, heterogeneous public school classroom. Just as much damage can be done by a teacher of such a class who holds back or does not challenge the leaders as by a teacher who neglects to provide for the needs of the slower children. Beware of being comforted by some mysterious "average" aptitude figure. There is no "average" child. He does not actually exist. Remember the statistician who went in over his head and drowned in a lake that was reported to have an average depth of three feet! What any homeroom teacher can strive for is a minimum standard of achievement for her class below which no one will find himself at the end of the year. On the other hand there should be no level above which a teacher wouldn't rejoice to see a child go. The stating of these desirable attitudes is far easier than for teachers to achieve them! The goals remain worthwhile and are no less worthy because they may not always be reached. As the poet has said, "No man should plan his dwelling below the level of the stars."

Up through the fourth grade foundations in the basic skills are the essentials. It is not essential that much time be spent on the social studies and on science at these levels if the basic skills of reading and number manipulation have not been achieved. Intensive work and considerable time must be spent with each child who has not acquired the mastery of skills expected of him. Of course nothing in the education of a child excludes anything else. In social studies, he should be increasing his reading power.

Working on a science unit should involve him in the use of mathematics. If his skills in reading and numbers are weak, however, he will not get the full benefit of the social studies or science lessons, and he will not be exposed to the intensive training he desperately needs in reading and mathematics.

For teachers whose interests incline them toward a particular academic subject, K-4 is not recommended. These are the areas for the generalist and not the specialist who wishes also to be a homeroom teacher. The principal concern of teachers at these levels is the perfection of the reading and number skills.

There is another important factor to consider when choosing on what level to teach. That is the age and maturity level of the children. First grade children's characteristics are different from fourth grade children's characteristics. To teachers and to parents these differences are real and important. The "feelings" of teachers and parents for the differences are based on more than emotional judgments. Arnold Gesell and Frances Ilg of the Yale Clinic of Child Development made exhaustive and painstaking observations of children from infancy to adolescence. In a book published by Harper Brothers in 1946, *The Child from Five to Ten,* they record the differences among the children observed in ten major fields of behavior: 1) Motor characteristics, 2) Personal hygiene, 3) Emotional expression, 4) Fears and dreams, 5) Self and sex, 6) Interpersonal relations, 7) Play and pastimes, 8) School life, 9) Ethical sense and 10) Philosophic outlook. The span of five to ten years is roughly the same as kindergarten through the fourth grade.

The years from five to ten occupy a middle position in [the child's] long span of immaturity. These middle years are intermediate both in a biological and a cultural sense. During them the child sheds his milk teeth, a biological event. At six years he cuts his first permanent tooth, a molar at that. We call it a school-entrance molar for it punctuates his induction into the elementary school system, which is a sociological event. . . .

Five, therefore, is a model age. For a brief period the child remains in a phase of balanced adjustment to himself and to his environment. It is as though his problem of development had been solved. But the push of growth and the pressure of cultural demands builds up new tensions. Sometimes these demands are excessive. It is as though the culture were bent on appropriating the child. He on his part is also bent on assimilating the culture; because, of course, he is destined to graduate from his five-year-oldishness.

It is not, however, easy to strike a smooth and steady balance between himself and his multifarious environment. At six years, he seems less integrated than he was at three years. He is more like the 2½-year-old child, who has not fully found either himself or his environment and is therefore in a fluctuating two-way equilibrium. The 6-year-old likewise is in a bipolar phase, trying at one and the same time to find himself and to find out his new environment. Choice and reconciliation between the two poles create tensions and hesitations. He is solving new problems of development. This is the key to understanding some of his difficulties and instabilities at the threshold of his formal education.

The 7-year-old has himself better in hand. He shows less lability [use of the mouth], and a greater capacity to absorb and organize his new cultural experiences. He establishes more firm relationships with his companions and his teacher. He is decidedly more unipolar. He is better able to take what comes. There is less disequilibrium. This is, comparatively speaking, an absorptive and assimilative phase. Day by day he grows in mental stature.

By the age of eight, the budget of income and outgo shows new balances. The child has built up a firmer body of experience and is able to give as well as to take. He shows more initiative and spontaneity in going out to meet the environment. He can fraternize with his co-equals. At nine he is detaching himself still more from the apron strings, and domestic tethers. With a mounting indifference to his elders when he is away from them he dwells in a culture of his own selection.

By the age of nine and ten this indifference reaches new heights. Boys and girls alike are amazingly self-dependent. Their self-reliance has grown, and at the same time they have acquired intensified group feelings. Identification with the juvenile group promotes the complex process of detachment from the domestic family group. This is part of the method of maturing.

At the same time the divergence between the two sexes is widening. By the age of ten, the tendency toward segregation is well defined. Girls, somewhat earlier than boys, enter upon the pre-pubertal period, marked by changes in body proportions, metabolism and endocrine secretions. These changes become yet more marked during adolescence, which is a prolonged period of diminishing immaturity. The child thus becomes a youth, the youth an adult.

Do you know yourself well enough to know what age you would prefer to teach? The uncertain six-year-old, stimulated and intrigued on the one hand by the world about him and frightened and confused on the other hand by his awareness of it is indeed different from the self-reliant ten-year-old who lives "in a culture of his own selection."

FIFTH AND SIXTH GRADES

In the fifth and six grades the majority of children will be between ten and twelve years of age. Most of the girls and many of the boys will consider themselves adolescents. Children of this age do not want to seem dependent on the teacher, although they will need and often seek help.

It is at this age also that the girls begin to show a far greater interest in their studies than the boys do. Boys become impatient with class work and look to sports for an outlet. There is a story about a fifth grade teacher who asked her class to make a list of great Americans. While the class was writing, the teacher stopped at Johnny's desk and asked if he had finished. "Not quite," Johnny replied scratching his head, "I can't decide on a fullback." Johnny, like most boys of his age, knew who he thought was important!

Intellectual stimulation and challenge is what children this age should have and what they will expect. Although some will still badly need instruction in the basic skills, for the most part a teacher can emphasize evaluation of what is read, rather than skill in reading, style of composition rather than the mechanics of grammar. Which is not to say that grammar, spelling, and comprehension will not have to be formally taught at this time. Of course they will, but such instruction should be almost wholly in a supporting rather than a prime role.

Subject matter will become increasingly important. Social studies and science will share equal time and emphasis with English and mathematics. Many school districts will have introduced the study of a foreign language, some as early as the third grade. It will be possible to exchange homerooms with fellow teachers. If your particular interest is history, you can often arrange to teach another homeroom in social studies while your homeroom is being taught science.

The controlling factors for your choice at these grade

levels will be your interest in the increasing emphasis on subject matter and your sympathy and empathy with this age group.

SEVENTH AND EIGHTH GRADES

In many public school districts the upper elementary grades have been incorporated into a junior high or middle school. Organizations of 6th-9th, 7th-9th, 6th-8th, and 7th-8th can be found. There are still many public school districts whose elementary schools include the eighth grade but it is rare, except in small rural districts, for the functional homeroom teacher plan to continue through the eighth grade. There may be the designation "homeroom teacher," but the function of such a person is to take attendance at the beginning of the day, possibly have a homeroom period in the course of the day, and probably teach the homeroom group one academic subject during the day. For the students their "homeroom" is where they report to school and where they keep their books and possibly their clothes. They would look to their homeroom teacher to give them official announcements, and to be involved in the preparation of their report card. Counseling aspects of a homeroom teacher's function vary in different schools from nonexistent through perfunctory and routine to a service of considerable importance. In the latter circumstance, the school district will have reduced the teaching load of the teacher so that scheduled conference periods can be held with students and with parents.

Even if the seventh and eighth grades are still a part of the elementary school, for all practical purposes the teachers are subject matter teachers. The accelerating trend in the last few years has been to move "down" into the seventh and eighth grades levels of study that formerly were taught only in high school — in mathematics, algebra and geometry; in science, general science, earth science, and traditional biology. It is becoming the rare seventh or eighth grade that does not offer Latin and modern foreign languages. In English, literature is being read at this level that not too many years ago was reserved for high schools, such as *Julius Caesar* and *A Tale of Two Cities*. Social studies at this level is more formal than in previous years. You will now find courses offered in economic geography, ancient history, and state histories, to name only a few.

Many students at these levels are in their teens. The boys are in that stage, bewildering to themselves and to those that love them, of believing themselves at one moment to be a man and at the next moment being confronted with their boy-ness. It is not an easy time. They often seek help and cannot find it. Their humor varies between the smart-aleck and the crude. Nevertheless, there is usually an element of shrewdness and honesty in it, as in the case of Tom who was being scolded by his mother for his low grades. "Robert doesn't get D's and C's does he?" "No," Tom admitted, "but he's different. He has very bright parents."

The girls at this age, on the other hand, are usually

quite confident that they are young women, and seek for social life among older boys, thereby bewildering still further the boys of their own age with whom they have been classmates for the past seven or eight years! Because they have "moved up into another social culture," and because they are still young in years and lack experience, girls of this age may be faced with heart-rending problems caused by social rejection, lack of sophistication, and standards of conduct and morals designed for much older persons.

Dedicated teachers are in great demand at this level. Too often those who teach children of this age wish to teach in high school and will transfer when they find an opening. No level of teaching requires more talent, more understanding, more physical strength, or a greater sense of humor than the top elementary grades. To repeat, each level of teaching is of equal importance to the growth of the child. Each level of teaching makes its own and special demands on the teacher. Only you can decide at what level you can perform the greatest service and fulfill your own needs with the greatest satisfaction.

4 Discipline

DISCIPLINE is not a set of rules. If you are a good teacher and your students are learning, true discipline will have been achieved. How can this happen? Let's take two teachers, one from a "difficult" neighborhood, and the other from a neighborhood much like the one you grew up in, who both provided true discipline for their classes.

An elementary teacher of a fifth grade class in a big city, in a district that drew the majority of its children from the truly culturally deprived, had been concerned all year with the discipline in her class. Almost half of her students were physically large, overage boys. Their interest in class work was spasmodic at best. It seemed to the teacher that she had spent an inordinate amount of time taking one or another of her "children" to the principal's office. As she thought back over the year that particular morning, she was convinced she had been a failure as a teacher because she had had too many disciplinary problems. Surely if she had been a better teacher, she would have prevented more of these incidents. She would have been able to reach these students and convince them of the importance of the class work.

She was thinking about this on this particular morning because of the presence of a "visiting principal" in her classroom. It was the practice in this school district for principals of schools who needed replacement teachers for the next year to visit the classrooms of teachers who had indicated a desire to change schools. In her classroom, therefore, on this morning in the spring term appeared a visitor who placed himself at a desk and began making notes on what he observed. There had been other visitors from time to time during the year, but the students in the class had never paid any attention to the strangers and had conducted themselves, for good or bad, very normally!

Today, the teacher sensed an unnatural quiet, an unnatural alertness to questions, and an exhibition of total decorum. So special was the atmosphere that the teacher became apprehensive. Something was afoot, an explosion might be building up. She prayed a little to herself that whatever was going to happen would take place after the visiting principal had left. At the recess break, the guest came to her desk and complimented her on her conduct of the class.

No sooner had he gone than the leader of the boys in this fifth grade class, a six-foot sixteen-year-old boy, whom on one or two occasions the teacher had taken to the principal for being involved in some violent action or other, came up to the desk and explained that he had noticed "the man," whom he guessed was someone from the "head office." The class did not want anybody giving bad marks to "their" teacher. The boy leader went on to say that he had passed the word around that *"teach"* was to get no hard times that morning. "You've been on the level with us all year. We think you're O.K. Mrs. Donaldson. We're not about to have any 'boss man' putting the tag on our 'teach,' " he confided, with a reassuring wink. Having said this, he asked, somewhat anxiously, "How'd we do 'teach'?" The bewildered teacher was only able to stammer out "Fine, fine, Joe," as she fought to keep back the tears.

The point of this real life story is that this teacher had achieved, without knowing it, true discipline in her class — respect for her fairness and judgment as a teacher, and affection for her as a person because the students knew she cared about them. By her more conventional, and up to then less experienced standards, she had thought that she had failed.

Discipline is achieved when the atmosphere in the classroom, the rapport between teacher and students, and the interaction of student with student and student with teacher creates a "climate" of attitude that enables learning to take place. The teacher who is competent to teach, who is fair and impartial toward her students, and who is straightforward and honest in her approach to problems and in her answers to questions will have good discipline.

The teacher who is poorly trained, who is not competent as a teacher, who employs sarcasm or ridicule with students, who plays favorites, who is indecisive in her decisions and who constantly changes the rules, does not have discipline in her class, no matter how silent the class may be from the beginning of the day to the close! One noted authority in elementary education used to warn his class of college students, "When you go into a class where every child is at his desk, where everything in the room appears to be neat and in its place, where not a sound can be heard, beware of it, for the chances are that nothing in the way of education is taking place!" In other words, silence and apparent orderliness do not of themselves indicate that there is true discipline. Silence and orderliness are appropriate at times and their existence will not, on the other hand, always exclude or prevent learning!

No one who has ever thought about being a teacher has failed to think about how to handle discipline. No one at this point has not felt a bit apprehensive. More of the apprehension comes from an uncertainty as to what discipline is. A gnawing feeling persists that keeping "order" is not all there is to it. It could not be that simple!

As an individual, try thinking about discipline and what

it will mean to you, try to remember how the teachers handled it who were admired and loved when you were a child. The picture is probably vague. Yes, you can recall one or two dramatic, horrifying or amusing incidents, but only because they were so unusual, so startling.

Such incidents were not typical of that class which your beloved Miss Chapin conducted in your fourth grade year. In fact, thinking about that class you remember the excitement of anticipation of each day, the warmth of praise when it came for a job well done, the firmness when a job was not well done, the obvious interest to hear of some "discovery" you had made, the understanding that Miss Chapin expressed when you had a problem or were in trouble. All of these memories are vivid and pleasurable to recall, but what rules there were for discipline or for conduct you cannot remember. You can still remember the awe but not fear, and the respect, affection, and love you had for this great teacher. How did Miss Chapin accomplish such good discipline in her class? That she surely had, for no one ever planned to misbehave or to displease her.

To begin with, Miss Chapin had gone to a state normal school, had been well trained at that time, but she continued to strengthen her training and broaden her education throughout her life. Not only had she kept up with the professional developments in education but she kept up with daily events in the world and in the community. She was competent, in other words, to do the job for which she was employed by the school district. She was more competent every year for she never stopped learning. She never expected to know all there was to know about teaching fourth grade children, but this very attitude was what kept her young in spirit. She never felt embarrassed to say "I don't know," and she never tired of trying to find out what she didn't know.

Miss Chapin was always on time. Miss Chapin made a point of coming to her classroom a half hour before the school officially opened, so that she was ready to greet the children when they arrived. She usually sat on a very low chair by the door so that she was at eye level with the children when they greeted her. During the day she always had her class lined up and ready when it was time for them to be taken to the physical education class, to go to the play yard for recess, or to go down to the cafeteria for lunch.

Her assignments for the next day were always written up on the board in the same location so that the children became accustomed to look in a familiar place. She also announced the assignment for the next day well before the class ended and the dismissal bell had rung. There never was any confusion when assignments were given out. There was always time for questions.

Lesson plans were always made up so that if Miss Chapin was sick and missed a class, which rarely happened, the substitute could carry on without a waste of the children's time. If a child was sick, proper assignments were prepared and delivered to the home by a fellow student or by some other means, so no child ever felt the desperation of being left behind, or of being forgotten. In Miss Chapin's class, because she was always on time, there was always time for the children.

Although you probably don't remember the style of Miss Chapin's clothes, you do remember that she always looked neat, clean and fresh. In fact, although it would have surprised Miss Chapin and would not have been true in the conventional use of the word, you thought she looked pretty! Somehow her style of dress never got in the way of what was going on in the class. It never distracted anyone by being sloppy on the one hand or flashy on the other. Her appearance, in short, was pleasing, appropriate, and of the fashion. By her appearance, as you think about it now, Miss Chapin contributed to the atmosphere, the climate, the mood, yes, in fact, to the discipline of the class.

Miss Chapin's voice, that is its tone, its quality, its accent and its warmth, is something you remember well. You can never remember hearing her strain her voice unnaturally. If there was loud talking going on among the children, Miss Chapin would never say "Class, be quiet." She always said, addressing directly the noisiest, "John, not so loud," or "Betty, lower your voice." There was another teacher you remember, who under similar circumstances would beg the class, "Please be quiet." It was rare that any child, particularly if they were in the midst of an interesting argument, associated the teacher's plea with himself. In fact as her voice became louder on successive attempts to gain order, he found it necessary to raise his own voice so that his fellow discussant, who probably was sitting several seats away, could hear his convincing argument. In no time at all in that class no one could work or accomplish anything. You did not look forward to going to that class. You sensed that you would be frustrated, irritated and overly tired by the end of the day.

When Miss Chapin spoke, you listened because she had something to say that was important to you. Furthermore, what she said was interesting and would be helpful. You liked the tone of her voice. It never threatened, it never hurt, it never sounded over-sweet or silly. Her words were clearly understood. Her voice could be warm, it could be firm, it could be encouraging, and it could be gay and responsive to a joke. Oddly enough Miss Chapin's accent was rather nasal and "out state" but that was the way Miss Chapin was. It was natural for her. You were happy to be in her class and proud of the way she was. Anything "different" from what you were used to at home, such as an accent, would have been a cause for ridicule in another, but with Miss Chapin it was a badge of honor.

The more you think about it and try to remember, the more you are convinced that there were very few stated rules or procedures. The ones that existed were all designed to make your life easier, unlike so many rules you had known and still encounter that seemed designed to prevent you from doing something that was natural and proper. As you recall it now there were sensible arrangements for checking out of the room to go to the washrooms and to go to the library for a book. There was a good system for storing your overcoat and overshoes on a winter's day. You liked the way guests to the class were taken care of. All these procedures seemed to make it easier for you to do what had to be done and at the same time create the least possible disturbance to the rest of the class.

Somehow in Miss Chapin's class the "show-offs" never seemed to take over. No one was able to get off the track of the discussion that was going forward. The lesson plan of the day proceeded in an orderly way. Curiously enough this happened even though more children spoke and had something to say in Miss Chapin's class than in any other class you can remember. Miss Chapin gave everybody a chance to be heard, in fact encouraged some of the class who were a bit shy to contribute their thoughts, but the "show-off" never got started. After a while the "show-off" no longer existed as such. He became a regular member of the class.

One teacher you remember had been a Wave during the war. Her class soon discovered that if any mention was made of the war, of the Waves, of women's part in the armed services, of military discipline, this teacher would be off on a series of personal experience stories. It was sort of fun to get her started, and kind of useful if there was a test scheduled to have her take so much time so that it had to be postponed, but before long these accounts became boring, particularly when they were repeated. You didn't look forward to going to this class the way you had to Miss Chapin's. Worst of all you made fun of this teacher and were not proud to be in her class. Her knowledge of military discipline did not help run her class; in fact, this class lacked any semblance of true discipline.

Discipline is achieved by the presence of many factors. The influence of any one factor varies with each class and will vary as applied to each child. In fact, you can say that even with one class or with one child what may be important today will have less importance tomorrow, for do not forget that each child is learning every day, growing every day, and therefore changing every day. Since this is so for each child, then collectively it becomes true for the class. The child and the class are not the same in June as they appeared to be in September. Nothing could be more foolish than to have a set approach to discipline or to learning applied regularly each year to each new class, and never varied from the beginning of the year to the end. What could have been a fine situation at the opening of school can deteriorate completely by the winter term if no sensitivity is shown to the nature of the change that has taken place. For change there will have been!

When someone knows you well and cares about you, there is little desire or need to misbehave. Rules and regulations do not seem to be necessary. With Miss Chapin and the other good teachers that you have had, you knew that they considered you as a person, a unique being. You probably felt secretly, as did every other member of the class, that you were Miss Chapin's favorite, but, of course, she couldn't acknowledge that. Somehow that made your secret all the more precious! Only you and Miss Chapin shared it.

What you have discovered since is that Miss Chapin spent a lot of time after school hours learning a great deal about you and each of the other children in her class. There were the reports from your previous teachers, the results of the tests you had taken, the findings of your annual medical examination, your standing on the physical fitness tests, and the information and impressions she had gotten talking to your parents. If you were heartbroken because your dog had been run over, Miss Chapin gave you comfort. If you were all excited because your daddy had been promoted or honored in some way, Miss Chapin rejoiced with you. You expected Miss Chapin to know all about you and to care about you. It never even occurred to you under these circumstances that you could be a disciplinary problem or that the class could cause trouble. Miss Chapin, you now understand, had true discipline in her class!

5   Teachers of the Exceptional Child

TEACHING exceptional children is a very rewarding and expanding field. In public school districts throughout the country it includes the orthopedically handicapped, the deaf and partially deaf, the blind and the partially blind, the aphasic, and the mentally retarded — both the educable and those considered only trainable.

Attempts have been made to define, in the legal sense, emotionally disturbed children so that they could receive special treatment in public schools or in public supported institutions. So far these attempts have not been too successful, and severely disturbed children are often treated by mental hospitals for the insane, while less severe cases are kept in the schools without expert attention. There are opportunities for work with the mentally disturbed, however, and they will be described in this chapter.

For years handicapped children were ignored by public schools throughout the United States. In some states efforts were made to operate schools for the deaf, the blind and the mentally retarded. Tragically, in the latter category children were often placed in mental institutions designed for adults, where there were no specially trained teachers and where the staff was so overburdened that little more than physical care could be given the children. There were isolated cases of big city school districts attempting to do something for the handicapped, but it is only within the last ten years that an increased awareness on the part of the public has led to a serious approach to the problem in general. Small school districts throughout the United States still do not have the money to cope with it. Even if they had sufficient funds, they probably could not find personnel properly trained to deal with the handicapped of their particular districts, where there would be relatively few cases, of perhaps very different categories.

In 1959 the school district of St. Louis County, Missouri, a county-wide district with its own tax base and administrative board and officers, was organized for handicapped children. For the first time, an integrated program, using the very best techniques, was available. This and one or two other special districts have been pioneers in a field which is now growing rapidly. Some Federal funds have always been available for particular research and experimental projects in this area. State funds are beginning to be made available, but most important as far as the rapid advance of this kind of education is concerned is the organization of comprehensive districts including many local school districts.

Dr. Morvin A. Wirtz, Director of the Division of Handicapped Children and Youth in the Department of Health, Education and Welfare in the Office of Education in Washington, D.C., who was the first superintendent of the special district for the handicapped in St. Louis County, described the kind of person he felt was best qualified to teach handicapped children.

First of all, I looked for young people fresh out of school from good solid training programs. Because of the dynamic kinds of things going on in special education I do not feel that we could afford to load up with individuals who were too firmly established in their habits and teaching patterns. I would always prefer to take a young person and give him final touches of training by supplying competent supervisory personnel to work with him.

Secondly, I would look for individuals who have demonstrated their flexibility. About ten years ago, I did an informal study on the relationship of rigidity to the success of teaching special education. I discovered that individuals who showed great rigidity tended to be poor teachers. This is an item which needs intensive exploration, but there is enough evidence to indicate that this certainly is a factor in success in teaching special education and may be true for education in general.

Thirdly, I looked for people who are ambitious and have a potential for developing into something other than a classroom teacher. This does not mean to say that I did not want these people to stay in the classroom but I tried to find people who are ambitious and the only way they could express their ambition was to wish to become a principal or a supervisor or something of this nature. Naturally, I also wanted, along with this, to develop the status of classroom teaching so that these people would receive the status they needed by staying in the classroom and doing an excellent job. This, of course, gets involved in our salary schedule structure, interpersonal relationships, and all of the other factors which go into luring bright young people out of the classroom.

Fourthly, I looked at the people who are willing to make a commitment for more than just one year. I recognized that this was not always possible because of contract problems but at least I wanted to explore with them their plans for the next five years.

It is evident from Dr. Wirtz's statement that attitude, intelligence, sympathy and imagination are far more important than any particular type of training. It is also true that a strong background in psychology, both normal, abnormal, and that involved specifically with the handicapped, will be an excellent part of the training of anyone who plans to go into the special education field. As we have indicated, there are many different categories of handicap. Each person should decide for himself what area he wishes to concentrate upon.

Besides the growing opportunities in public school districts, there are many private institutions of international reputation, such as the Orthogenic School at the University of Chicago directed by Dr. Bruno Bettelheim, and the Institute for the Deaf in St. Louis, where exciting work has been going on for years.

MENTALLY RETARDED

The world that we take for granted is a noisy, fast-moving and confusing place for the child afflicted with any degree of mental retardation. No one really knows how the world does appear to these children. All we are sure of is that when exposed to the normal pace of family and community life they become apprehensive and frightened. The result can vary between total withdrawal and violent, aggressive actions. Because the pace of a school for the healthy, normal child reflects, and sometimes even intensifies, the rate of daily living, it is no place for the mentally retarded. These children should be segregated, particularly in the early years, with children of similar low aptitude, and a "bland atmosphere" should be created for them. For example, in the Clarke School for mentally retarded youngsters in St. Louis County there was once a mentally retarded janitor, who performed his job most effectively. He could cope with the children of this school and they with him. It was a happy school for there was no competition; the speed of life was suited to those who learned and worked there. The rate of learning was less rapid than in many schools, but there was a measurable degree of development. The satisfactions for the teachers were comparable to those enjoyed by all teachers.

Children who are mentally retarded have extremely short attention spans, and usually lack the physical co-ordination of normal children. Dressing themselves and going up and down stairs loom as major problems that have to be mastered. Art and music has a special place in the school life of a retarded child. Finger painting, when you have trouble grasping a crayon or a brush, is far more direct and brings quicker satisfactions. Music can be used in many ways. Songs help in acquiring some ability to memorize. Music also helps to quiet and soothe anxieties that some of the children are prey to from time to time.

EMOTIONALLY DISTURBED

Unfortunately, there is a confusion in the popular mind between the mentally retarded or handicapped and the emotionally disturbed. One authority, Norris G. Haring, has defined emotionally disturbed children as those who have more or less serious problems with other people (both of their own age and their parents and teachers), or who are unhappy and unable to apply themselves according to their abilities and interests. The significant thing about this definition is that emotionally disturbed children have abilities and interests within the normal range. They have not been born with certain physical defects that characterize the mentally handicapped. Misunderstandings have occurred because the outward symptoms of withdrawal, irrational behavior, overly aggressive actions, tears and hysteria are exhibited by mentally retarded children and also by children who may have considerable mental ability and aptitude but who, for one or for many of a number of psychological reasons are emotionally disturbed.

Furthermore, just as there is a wide variety of degree of mental retardation, there is a tremendous difference in the seriousness of emotional disturbances. By love and understanding, patience and firmness, what may appear to be a serious emotional problem can many times be lifted and the child will become free and happy like other children.

Bobby had announced to the new fourth grade teacher on the first day that he did not like school. When she suggested that this year might be different and he would enjoy school, he stomped off to his desk without replying. The teacher had noticed that he always came to school with a briefcase which he obviously prized. It appeared to be a status symbol to him. He kept it by his side all the time, as though no matter how much he disliked school or how poorly he might do in his lessons, his briefcase set him apart and made him special. Occasionally Bobby would look into his briefcase and then snap it shut with obvious satisfaction.

One day after a month of school, Bobby left his briefcase at school when he went home. The teacher was quite concerned that he would be miserable without it. She called home to alert the family but there was no answer. She stayed after school an extra hour in case he came back or there was a telephone call. Next morning with some apprehension she watched Bobby come in. He went to his desk but paid no attention to the briefcase.

This went on for several days. It seemed to the teacher that Bobby was playing more with the other children. He even appeared more friendly towards her. She hardly dared admit this to herself for she wished so much for it to be true!

One evening in cleaning up the room the janitor placed the briefcase on a small table by her desk. Although it was in plain sight, Bobby paid no attention to it. By Christmas vacation the briefcase had been relegated to a corner of the room, forgotten by Bobby and by the teacher. As Bobby left to go home for vacation, he came up to the teacher and wished her a "Happy Christmas," but even more wonderful were the words, "I'll see you after New Year's!"

To the teacher Bobby's transformation was a miracle. As the room took on the unnatural quiet that only an empty classroom in a schoolhouse without children can achieve, she thought of Bobby's briefcase. She went over to the corner and picked it up. An overwhelming desire swept over her to open it and see what treasure had meant so much to Bobby. She undid the clasp and looked in. It was empty!

Now the teacher knew that somehow in her class Bobby had found something to take the place of the emptiness. It was no longer important for him to have a "crutch," a status symbol. He had found a meaning to his life in the school with his classmates and with the teacher.

A number of methods of dealing with seriously disturbed children are being practiced today. At one extreme is the Orthogenic School at the University of Chicago which is directed by Dr. Bruno Bettelheim. The philosophy of this school, according to Haring and Phillips, is "providing the avenues for children to bring into consciousness their unconscious repressions." This method can be generalized as the psychoanalytic approach. At the other extreme is a structural approach, with a planned routine that was devised originally for brain-damaged children. In between are such methods as the nondirective-permissive approach and the child-study approach. All of these methods overlap at one point or another. From an economic point of view which governs public schools to a large extent, the more individual program, such as that found at the Chicago Orthogenic School, is likely to be the most costly and therefore least practical. Sadly, emotional problems are *totally individual* to the person afflicted, so that group therapy and group teaching can at best be only partly successful.

THE DEAF AND THE BLIND

In both categories of deaf and blind, basic intelligence is represented by a normal curve. A teacher must be trained in special techniques essential for proper performance. However, other than the use of special materials and equipment, the problems of teaching the deaf and the blind are similar to the problems faced by all teachers. Just as much interest is expressed by a deaf or a blind child when he discovers the Amazon River from the study of a unit on South America as by a child in a regular fourth grade class.

ORTHOPEDICALLY HANDICAPPED

A ten-year-old boy was strapped into a chair so that he would not fall out. His arms and legs were not sufficiently developed to be in any way helpful to him. In front of him was a fixed easel with a pad of composition paper secured to it. Suspended from a band around the boy's head was a pencil placed at the end of a wire so that by moving his head he could write on the pad. He was writing about a trip to the zoo he had taken the day before. Another boy with similar handicaps was reading a book and turning the pages by means of an ingenious contraption which he could operate by tripping a lever with a rod attached to his head band.

These two boys were very intelligent, judged by any of

the standard aptitude tests. Miracles are occurring every day in schools designed for the orthopedically handicapped. With the physically handicapped of any kind — deaf, blind, orthopedic — there is total devotion to the task before them. A blind bandmaster of a brass band of blind children explained, when complimented on the quality of the music, "It is not that we have such extra special talents as musicians, it is that we are not distracted or tempted by other things. We give all our energy and time to practice and to playing!"

Are there any special characteristics that a teacher of cripples should possess? Experts who have taught the orthopedically handicapped believe that teachers must have an education with breadth and depth enough to give them understanding of the psychology of a crippled child. In his book called *Orthopedics for the Teachers of Crippled Children,* Dr. Samuel Boorstein had this to say about qualifications:

Her greatest task will lie in combatting the mental attitude which crippledom has inflicted on the child. While it is true that in general the parents no longer look with contempt or even hatred on the deformed (the child is no longer called "lame brat" as was Lord Byron), in the great majority of cases the mother does find him a troublesome burden on her hands and cannot give him the attention and care he needs. And then on the other hand, he occasionally becomes the favorite, and the mother, and not infrequently the father, attempts with lavish affection and acquiescence to every whim, to make up for nature's handicap, or fate's ill turn. The result is naturally a cranky, selfish, domineering child, cordially disliked, if not actually hated by the other members of the family. The neighbors' children, his playmates are even less likely to tolerate these traits, and the child is thrown back on himself. . . . It would hardly be exaggerating the case to say that the entire future of the child may depend on the teacher he encounters. The teacher must take a personal interest in him, must become his friend, his confidante, must show him at every opportunity with stories or books and photographs that many cripples have made a success of life. Such examples as Alexander the Great, Milton, Byron, Helen Keller, Steinmetz, and President Franklin Roosevelt forcibly illustrate that a brilliant personality may be housed in a crooked or defective physical body. To carry out these ideas and at the same time cope with a mind predisposed to inferiority complex, this teacher must possess much more patience than the ordinary teacher, must be kind and must have a real natural fondness for children. Those entering this field who do not possess these qualities, can never hope to succeed and will certainly never be happy in their work.

Over and over again in the books about teaching children with handicaps emphasis is placed on the vital importance of the teacher and her understanding of the psychology and condition of the children. Two movies have skillfully demonstrated this point. *The Miracle*

Worker is about the childhood of Helen Keller, who was both blind and deaf — but the worker of miracles was her teacher, Miss Anne Sullivan. *David and Lisa* is concerned with two emotionally disturbed teenagers who find themselves and each other through the wise guidance of the director of the "home" in which they have been placed.

6 Specialists

THIS chapter describes the special fields of physical education, guidance, speech therapy, reading, home tutoring, music, art, and the academic specialties at the elementary level of foreign languages, mathematics, and science.

The homeroom teacher in her self-contained classroom is becoming a rare person. One or more specialists takes over her class a number of times a week. No grade level is immune. Specialists can be found teaching in nursery school and all the way up to the eighth grade.

PHYSICAL EDUCATION AND HEALTH

Hardly any field of education has progressed more in the last thirty years than physical education. In the early days of the public schools, free play at recess constituted the only physical activity for the children during school time. Later, games were introduced and perhaps calisthenics or exercises. The latter were designed to develop different muscles and so could be termed the beginnings of physical education as a part of the planned curriculum. The concept of physical fitness, muscular control and skills evaluated by sophisticated tests and measurements did not exist then, any more than the overall goal of mental and physical health for each child.

Today teachers trained in physical education, working with a carefully planned curriculum, provide elementary children with a balanced program. Much of this desirable advance at the elementary level has been made possible not only by the highly skilled teachers and the scientific curriculum but also by the increasing number of gymnasiums, recreation rooms, swimming pools, and adequate playing fields now available in the schools for the younger children. There was a time when the only children in the public schools who received any supervised exercise were the athletes in high school — a group who needed physical education less than any other!

Today a teacher of physical education should understand thoroughly the physiological reasons for all the organized activities and the implied effects of these activities on the physical and mental health of the children. He or she should also be able to supplement the academic work of the classroom by carefully selected activities. For instance, if one of the grades is involved in a unit on Scotland a modification of the Scottish games can be introduced, stressing the physical skills needed and their relationship to the life and history of the Scots. In collaboration with the music teacher Scottish dances can be introduced.

In contests mathematics may be used in timing and measuring distances. The cultural significance of forms of exercise, games, contests, dances, and music are meaningful. The health aspects of physical education are inseparably related to almost every lesson in science at the elementary level. Literature about physical prowess and sports in our culture begins with the Greeks and continues right on down to the latest best seller or magazine article. Filmstrips, records, tapes, and motion pictures supply rich aids to any lesson.

As we have mentioned, testing and measurement of the results of physical activity have become highly developed. Teachers of physical education must understand the strengths and weaknesses of the tests used, what they are actually measuring, and the significance of the results to the individual's development and health. Every program of physical education should have well articulated testing and measurement procedures built into it.

What is taking place in the teaching of physical education is a return to the ancient Greek philosophy which emphasized that you cannot separate the activities of the mind from the activities of the body. Further, you cannot separate such activities from changing social systems and cultures. Edith Hamilton in *The Greek Way,* one of her superb books on ancient times, summed up this point of view: "But if ever a day comes when our intelligentsia is made up of our football players, we shall be on the way to understanding the Athenian . . ." and, we might add, a model of what modern man should be. Physical education and health are central to any good elementary school program. The daily period for physical education is a time for learning no less important to the welfare of the child than the lesson in language arts or any other academic subject.

GUIDANCE AND COUNSELING

The field of guidance and counseling in American education is relatively new. Only a few public school districts employ trained guidance counselors for the elementary grades, but the number is increasing.

The individual who is particularly interested in personality development and adjustment will find a position in guidance very challenging. This position at the elementary level requires knowledge and skill in administering and interpreting tests to teachers, principals, and parents. Based on the information gathered about a child, positive suggestions to benefit the child are made, ranging all the way from proceeding with the regular program to recommending that the child be referred to a psychiatrist for treatment.

In preparing yourself to be an elementary guidance counselor, you should emphasize in your college work psychology courses of various kinds, testing and measurement courses, statistics, and guidance courses. Furthermore, an awareness of reading problems, physical disabilities that can inhibit learning in school, and emotional conditions that affect children must be part of the background of a well-prepared counselor. Full-time guidance work is not recommended until the prospective counselor has taught for at least three years. Obviously there may be special situations where part-time work in guidance may be carried on together with a homeroom teaching assignment.

Guidance work is a growing and vital aspect of elementary education and offers interesting and varied opportunities for the individual going into teaching.

SPEECH THERAPIST

Sometimes called the speech correctionist, the speech therapist is now a certifiable specialist in over thirty states and is employed by school districts in a number of other states. These figures reflect the need that exists among children in our public schools.

Obviously if speech correction is to be provided by a school district it must be available early in a child's school life. When the basic correction and remedial work is left to the high school years it becomes a frustrating "patch-up" job.

Speech therapists must first diagnose each case to determine the seriousness and, if possible, the course of the trouble. In severe cases, referrals must be made to medical doctors or psychiatrists. As in the case of the school guidance counselor, therapists are not competent to treat medical ills — physical, emotional or mental. The therapist must determine as early as possible whether the defect is specific or whether it is symptomatic of something deeper.

The defects or handicaps that can and should be treated by a therapist are generally lisps (my thither Thue wath thick), sound substitutes (chimley for chimney, shursh for church, bwover for brother), and indistinct or careless speech.

What do college students do to train themselves as specialists in speech correction? They take courses in choral speaking, creative dramatics, interpretation, and public speaking. Child psychology, educational psychology, and knowledge of tests and their interpretation are included in their programs. Finally, specific courses in speech therapy and speech correction are an essential for anyone expecting to specialize. It will be necessary to determine which colleges offer such courses before you decide where to go.

Teaching of this kind at the elementary level has the added reward of helping children who have particular needs and who require special attention.

READING SPECIALIST

Reading is the basic ingredient of elementary schooling. When and how the child learns to read are of prime importance. Everyone who is being trained to teach at the elementary level receives instruction on how to teach reading. Why are reading specialists necessary under such conditions?

In one of the most thorough and competent books in print of reading, *Improving the Teaching of Reading,* Emerald V. Dechant writes: "The Latins had a phrase, *tot capita, tot sententiae* (so many people, so many opinions), that perhaps best describes our predicament when we seek to define reading. There are just about as many descriptions or definitions of reading as there are 'reading experts.' " The author lists eight characteristics that she believes are fundamental: (1) Reading is a sensory process; (2) Reading is a perceptual process; (3) Reading is a response; (4) Reading is a learned response; (5) Reading is a developmental task; (6) Reading can be an interest; (7) Reading is a learning process; (8) Reading is communication.

With all these elements involved in teaching to read, it is not hard to understand why even the best and most experienced elementary teachers are puzzled because some of their students are not learning to read as well as others. Recognizing that there are many ways of teaching reading, teachers seek the help of "experts" to criticize their approach and to suggest different approaches, much in the same way that the experienced artist benefits from criticism of his work by a master painter, or a top-flight golfer needs coaching now and then from a professional.

Reading specialists employed by a school district to concentrate at the elementary level will be consultants, that is they will work with teachers in what amounts to in-service training, and they will be directly teaching children remedial reading. Depending on the case load, some reading specialists may devote themselves to one of these two areas to the exclusion of the other.

Are any special characteristics required for success as a reading specialist? None that are not required for elementary teachers in general. The ability to work with others has more importance than might be true for a homeroom teacher who "runs her own show." The reading specialist will be dealing with pupils, other teachers, parents, supervisors, principals, even the superintendent.

Particular preparation for the position should include at least two years as a classroom teacher. More and more college programs for elementary teacher training are increasing the number of courses in reading.

The reading specialist needs to know and to understand all the different methods of teaching reading in order to help teachers in their particular situations. Over the years the most successful teachers have not adhered slavishly either to the "phonic" approach or to the "sight" approach; they have used both to advantage. John Gardner, then President of the Carnegie Corporation, summarized a conference of distinguished experts in the field of reading as follows:

It is my belief that the two sides in the argument over phonics are moving toward one another and that in the next few years the argument will become meaningless except for crackpots and zealots, of whom we'll always have a plentiful supply. A group of nationally known reading experts who met in New York last year — most of them *not* identified with the phonics movement — said in their draft report, "We consider phonics one of the essential skills that help children identify printed words that they have not seen before and to understand the meaning that those words represent. Without phonics children cannot become self-reliant, discriminating, efficient readers." — from "Learning to Read," a report published in 1962 by the Educational Testing Service.

Quantities of research and writing have been done on the teaching of reading. Special problems emerge reflecting the changing nature of the social order. In a household where there are many books on the shelves, where the parents read a great deal and where the children have been read to since infancy, children can learn to read by methods far different from those required for children whose homes contain no books, and whose parents have never read for enrichment or for entertainment.

The Augmented Roman Alphabet (A.R.A.), recently renamed the Initial Teaching Alphabet (i.t.a.), developed by Sir James Pitman of England, is one of the latest examples of an attempt to help children learn to read English. It is still too early to know positively that i.t.a. is of significant help to beginning readers, but from what evidence has been accumulated, the findings appear to fall on the plus side. There is considerable evidence that this method may help some slow reading learners and also that it is particularly helpful to the culturally disadvantaged and to foreigners learning to read English.

What is there special about i.t.a. and why is it significant? Over the years there has not only been endless exploration and heated debate as to whether the *phonic* method was better than the *sight* or *look-say* method, but there have been numerous attempts to "reform" English spelling (i.e., tho for though — a *Nue Speling*). It has even been proposed to replace the English language by a universally acceptable artificial language such as Esperanto, which was invented by Dr. Zamenhof, a Russian philosopher, in 1917. For many reasons, some practical, some political, and some emotional, these different "reforms" never attracted more than a handful of followers. For English-speaking people the basic problem has been that similar letter combinations are pronounced differently, and different letter combinations are pronounced the same. For example, lead, meaning to guide, and lead, the name of a metal, and in the second category, words such as blue, shoe, zoo, do.

Pitman increased the normal alphabet to forty-three characters so that all *phonemes* in English would be represented. He concentrated on making the words in i.t.a. similar to their form in traditional spelling. *The i.t.a. Reading Experiment,* an evaluation made in 1964 by John A. Downing of the University of London Institute of Education, Reading Research Unit, concludes that:

> The design and use of Pitman's special beginning reading alphabet has resulted in a high level of compatibility between English printed in i.t.a. and English in standard lower case print. This arises from the deliberate attempt to ease the transfer of reading skill from i.t.a. to conventional spelling which all children must make eventually if Pitman's aim of improving children's ability in reading *standard print* is to be achieved. . . . his basic objective is to enable children to learn *to read our traditional English spelling* with greater fluency, comprehension and competence.
>
> A second innovation in i.t.a. is that it is designed to give a new opportunity of raising standards of literacy *both* through the 'Look-Say' and through the 'Phonic' methods of teaching reading. 'Look-Say' teaching should be helped by i.t.a. because it removes the variations in visual patterns of words, and 'Phonic' teaching should be given a real chance of success by i.t.a. because it provides an adequate number of characters and uses them consistently.

The question of transferring over to standard English spelling from Pitman's alphabet is of major concern to teachers of beginning reading. On evidence not yet conclusive, gathered from observations made but not substantiated at the Laboratory Schools of the University of Chicago and by a number of researchers in England summarized by Downing, transfer to *reading* has taken place with comparative ease but transfer to *writing* traditional orthography (t.o.) has been somewhat more difficult for the children. From scattered observations made at Chicago it would appear that a significant number of students learning to read in i.t.a. find little trouble in reading in t.o. at home.

The i.t.a. approach is the first significantly new approach to beginning reading. It is a radical and imaginative invention which attacks at the roots the characteristics of the English language that have made beginning reading particularly difficult for English-speaking children. The worth of the method is still not conclusively proved by research. The scope and implications of its uses have only been tentatively explored. In England, where i.t.a. has been used longer and more widely than in the United States, the Office of Education in 1964, based on the evidence which they had accumulated, gave its approval for the use of i.t.a. in the tax-supported schools.

Anyone who has an interest in becoming a reading specialist should keep an open mind toward such methods as i.t.a., which appear to offer hope for helping children learn to read more easily.

HOME OR TUTORING TEACHER

Home or tutoring teachers are carried by many public school districts to provide on the one hand education for children who are bed-ridden and living at home, and on the other a "back-up" teacher who will schedule visits to schools to help children "catch up" with work missed because of illness or give remedial teaching for those who need extra assistance beyond what the homeroom teacher can provide. The advantages to the individual teacher of this type of position is the variety of the experience, the satisfaction that comes from helping those who have particular needs, the fact of being "on your own," and the opportunity, if this is important to you, of working less than full time or on special hours rather than a fixed schedule.

Preparation for this type of position should include a strong background of beginning reading and beginning mathematics, as well as some interest and competency in educational psychology. A broad liberal education should be the foundation.

MUSIC AND ART

If your interests are primarily in music or in art, there are many opportunities for the specialist in elementary schools. Your job will undoubtedly divide itself between helping teachers maintain music and art in their classrooms and working with children directly in fairly large groups.

In music, beginning with nursery school children, rhythms and tonal discriminations can be introduced and developed up through the elementary grades to the point of playing classical symphonic music with an orchestra of close to a hundred performers! Between these extremes every conceivable musical experience is possible. The low quality and unimaginative content of much musical offering at the elementary level is no fault of the students! Potential musical talent exists in any group of children. The responsibility for the program, good or bad, has to be borne by the teacher. "Rudolph the Red-Nosed Reindeer" in place of a lively and humorous Mozart piece is a decision the teacher makes for presentation to the P.T.A. meeting.

Research has revealed among healthy children that the incidence of "tone deafness" is negligible. A number of successful experiments have been carried out with first grade children who were declared to be monotones. Within a few months they were able to sing on key and derive satisfaction out of their musical experiences.

A major satisfaction for the music specialist should be the fact that there is no part of the curriculum, no point in the day of a homeroom class, where some form of musical expression is not appropriate. The successful music specialist is the one who will be able to cooperate with the homeroom teacher and other specialists by providing exciting and pertinent musical experiences that enforce and enrich the work in the classroom. For instance, in social studies music can aid in the understanding of the culture of the past and the conditions of the present. Music describes geographical and climatic conditions of various countries. Much of the history of a country is expressed through its music. Who will forget the significance of Sibelius's "Onward Ye People," the Finnish National Anthem, when the great railroad station in Helsinki was jammed with citizens singing their native anthem as they bid farewell to their Premier on his way to Moscow to negotiate a peace that would leave some integrity and honor to their country! In the music of Sibelius all the pride, all the hopes, all the joy, all the sadness of a small country resisting the onslaught of a large and ruthless nation was expressed. Surely in our country Negro spirituals, Western ballads, and jazz illuminate parts of our history more strikingly than many thousands of printed words. Yet social studies is only one area. The relationships of music to the language arts, mathematics, science, physical education and health, and art are countless.

To sum up, the music specialist can promote music by working directly with teachers and children in singing and instrument play. She can also relate her specialty in every way to the daily learning within the classroom.

A music specialist must have as much academic and performing music as possible in her training, and a better than average skill in playing the piano and some wind or stringed instrument. A broad liberal education will enable the music teacher to relate all areas of knowledge taught in elementary schools. A knowledge of educational psychology and the usefulness of music tests should complete her preparation.

The art specialist is in exactly the same relationship to the school, to the teachers, and to the children as the music specialist. If anything, there are more ways in art than in music to be involved with all aspects of the curriculum. Forms of art are everywhere, from the design of the spoon we use in the cafeteria to the reproduction on the classroom wall of one of Van Gogh's bridges at Arles. As in music, there are examples of bad art as well as good art on every hand. The development of taste, judgment, discrimination becomes a part of the responsibility of the music and art specialists.

Children hunger for art in its many forms and will create art for themselves by drawing, by making crude forms from mud or sand, by "acting out" plays, by singing or whistling tunes they have composed. This will take place in some form with every child. Children do not separate art from their daily lives in the way adults are accustomed to do. Children learn through art expression, and through it personality development evolves with greater force than in almost any other aspect of their daily lives.

The music and art specialists have instant rewards for their efforts. Take the case of the school boy who was asked to illustrate the song "America, the Beautiful." The teacher recognized the flag, the map, the "purple mountains," and even the youthful artist's idea of "from sea to shining sea." But she couldn't understand the airplane in one corner covered with red and yellow balls. "That," explained the 7-year-old artist, "is the fruited plane."

Since no way has yet been devised to predict artistic ability or degree of creativity, all children must be given an opportunity to develop their musical and artistic potential. To kill in the child the natural urge to express himself through some art form is to produce an inflexible and limited adult. The love and enthusiasm that the specialists in music and art reveal for their chosen fields will bring joy to the children, and can well contribute to high morale in a school.

THE ACADEMIC SPECIALISTS

The principal of the Demun Elementary School in Clayton, Missouri, was standing with his superintendent at the front of the school on a cold wintry morning while the children were arriving. As the two men stood there greeting or nodding to each child, they were joined by Mrs. Pei, the French specialist. One little third grade boy pushed open the heavy door and stomped his feet free of snow on the mat, pulled back his scarf from his face and looked up to see the three grown-ups standing in the hall. He smiled at the principal and greeted him with a cheery, "Good morning, Mr. Captain" and then looking at Mrs. Pei he said without hesitation, "Bonjour, Madame Pei," and went on down the hall to his classroom. Later in the morning, when the recess period had come, which in that school was a free time for the children to play as they wished, a number of children in the third and fourth grades were heard by the supervising teacher playing games in French.

How was it possible that third grade children in a typical American elementary public school in the Middle West would be at ease speaking French and taking advantage of opportunities to use the language outside the classroom? The answer is that in this school French was being taught to all children beginning with the third grade in a program called Fles (Foreign Languages in the Elementary School). The approach in this school was entirely oral until at least the fifth grade. From the very first class held with third graders only French was spoken, and some French was taught every day in each class. Although some homeroom teachers could handle the assignment, there were many who could not. A French specialist was therefore essential, to teach those sections where the homeroom teacher lacked the skill and knowledge, and also to coordinate the whole program and to develop materials as they were needed.

The general conditions that the academic subject matter specialist faces in elementary schools are similar in whatever subject area is chosen — foreign languages, mathematics, or science. The position of specialist gives the individual who enjoys the intellectual challenge of an academic subject, who finds satisfaction in teaching, who prefers to teach children of elementary age, and who likes to innovate and experiment, a chance to have several cakes and to munch on all of them!

There are those who question the need and desirability of emphasizing by the use of specialists the study of academic subjects at the elementary level. It cannot be denied that the entrance into a classroom, if for only one period, of a specialist reduces by that much the time the homeroom teacher has with her class. The decision that has to be made by school administrators is whether the loss of time with the grade teacher is better employed by the acquisition of time by the specialist. If certain bodies of knowledge are now thought to be desirable for elementary children to acquire, and in many cases the concern is for the college-bound, academically talented child, can a homeroom teacher be competent in them all? The plus and minuses involved must be evaluated by the administration of the school. Nationally, the trend would appear to be an increasing demand for more and more qualified specialists who want to teach at the elementary level.

In a widely read book, *The Process of Education,* Jerome Bruner began the chapter "Reading for Learning" with this statement:

> We begin with the hypothesis that any subject can be taught effectively in some intellectually honest form to any child at any stage of development. It is a bold hypothesis and an essential one in thinking about the nature of the curriculum. No evidence exists to contradict it; considerable evidence is being amassed that supports it.

Preparation for an academic subject specialist will require a minimum of five years — four years of a liberal arts program with a major in the special subject and a year devoted to special methods and techniques necessary to teach at the elementary level. Practice teaching and a thorough knowledge of the materials available, and of the way to go about developing new materials, are highly desirable.

7 Independent Schools

LOCATED in a country setting with several acres of land, an attractive modern building, not too far distant from the center of the city, is the typical independent elementary country day school. Since the school is independent and has no "enrollment boundaries," it can draw children from any part of the city, and can make certain, if it cares to, that the children represent different racial, religious and ethnic groups. Within limits controlled by the amount of financial aid available, a fairly broad spread of economic background can be represented by the families of its students. For city-dwelling children, many of them living in apartments with no backyards to play in, such country day schools have tremendous appeal. Furthermore, in big cities certain areas are almost totally segregated in one form or another, and the schools serving these districts are segregated in the same way. By the very nature of public school district organization, they are forced into a particular mold, whereas an independent school is free to draw its students from any area, to have mixed races and religions, and to have foreign students if such arrangements are possible. The public schools, ironically enough, founded on democratic principles, sometimes do not promote the best interests of democracy!

For families who are constantly moving — army and navy, government officials, or employees of large international corporations — independent elementary boarding schools may be better answers than repeated changing of schools. Whether it be an independent day school in a city, a country day school, or an independent elementary boarding school, the costs to the family for tuition must be considered. What makes such schools seem desirable to parents?

Public schools operated and supported by tax monies are available to the children of every family and exist in every neighborhood. Every child in the United States is assured an education at least through the eighth grade or until he is sixteen years of age. Furthermore the law says that every child must go to school for at least this minimum span of

time and that he must begin when he is six years old at the
first grade level. As we have mentioned previously in this
book, public school districts are even offering kindergarten
education for those who wish it. In the big cities, particularly in the most congested areas, nursery schools are also
being operated by public monies in an attempt to close the
cultural gap between the newly arrived child from a remote rural area and the typical city-bred child.

To repeat, with such schools available to all children at
no extra cost, what reason can there be for tuition-sup-
ported independent or private schools? The answer is not
simple, nor can it be generalized except to state that for
a variety of reasons the families of children who attend independent schools believe these schools offer a more beneficial experience to their children than the community public schools can offer.

"Beneficial" can have such divergent meanings as a particular religious training at the same time as the academic
experience; a more demanding intellectual experience than
is thought possible in the neighborhood school; a specialized program of study that might give special emphasis to
art, music, dancing, drama or even to certain academic subjects; and a program designed for the handicapped, especially where the program is geared to a particular handicap, physical, mental or emotional.

"Beneficial" to the individual family sometimes has negative connotations. The main object may not be better or
more appropriate education but rather a belief that they
are socially "keeping up with the Joneses." Recently a

number of private schools have been organized for the sole purpose of preserving a segregated student body. Certainly reasons such as these are not concerned primarily with the worth of the educational offering.

In the largest category of independent schools is the religiously oriented school. The Roman Catholic Church operates parochial schools at a parish level through a diocesan organization. Almost all of the teachers in such schools are nuns. Separate from the diocesan organization but still under church supervision are schools run by particular orders — the Jesuits, the Benedictines and a host of others. Finally there are a few Roman Catholic schools that are organized by and are maintained by lay boards of trustees. In these schools more lay teachers are found than in the other types described. Because of the tremendous growth of Roman Catholic schools and the consequent shortage of "teaching sisters," more and more lay persons are teaching in them.

Many Protestant faiths run schools. The Lutherans have a parochial arrangement similar to the Roman Catholics but far smaller in number of schools. In most other Protestant churches the decision to organize a school is for the local parish to make. The Jewish faith, particularly the Orthodox elements, have well-organized schools.

Nursery schools, since few are supported by public money, are usually privately operated. Originally such schools were little more than organized baby-sitting, but increasingly they are being run by professional and scientific standards. Controlled play and personal interactions leading to concept formations are replacing the haphazard goings on of earlier times. Highly structured schools like those run according to Madame Montessori's philosophy are becoming more and more numerous.

Good independent elementary schools ranging from kindergarten through eighth grade exist in most communities of any size. They attempt to give a quality education weighted heavily on the side of the intellectual and academic. Another category of independent school that stresses innovation and experimentation together with quality is the laboratory school operated by private universities and colleges.

For children with exceptional talents in the arts, specialized schools can provide opportunities that no public school could possibly offer. This type of school is usually found only in large cities. They feature music, art, ballet, and acting. Others operate as foreign language schools, or as schools stressing mathematics and science.

Other types of specialized independent elementary schools operate according to the philosophies of Pestalozzi, Froebel, Dewey, or to more recent developments such as the "block" approach (one subject for an extended period of time). Since these schools are independent, they are free within certain prudent limits to promote whatever philosophy of education they believe in.

For handicapped children some independently operated schools are world-famous. Because they are able to limit the number of students they take and because they are able to get funds that enable them to spend significant amounts for each child enrolled, and finally because of their freedom to innovate and to experiment, they attract able and dedicated people to teach. Although there are indeed some fine publicly supported schools for the handicapped, the typical situation in public schools is overcrowding, understaffing, inadequate physical facilities, and insufficient funds.

In considering an independent private school as a place to teach, inquire about its organization. Proprietary schools are those which are owned by an individual or by a family. These schools are operated for a profit and as such are not exempt from taxation. Gifts to such a school, for instance would not be tax deductible. Schools organized "not for profit" are legally owned by a board of trustees and are tax-exempt. These are "independent" schools. The kind of organization does not guarantee a good school, however. There are good proprietary schools and extremely bad trustee-owned schools. Yet in general an organization "not for profit" has proven to be better for a school than a profit motive benefitting an individual or a family. The guiding principle of a school should be what is best for the education of children.

The second important point of inquiry should be concerning the school's accreditation. Public schools are subject to state regulations and state requirements. Within the range permitted by a particular state board of education, at least the minimum standards can be determined. Independent schools are not under the control of most state laws. However, responsible independent schools have their own organizations that set standards and evaluate their member schools. Usually a school must have been in existence for at least three years before it is eligible to apply for admission to such an accrediting organization.

The National Association of Independent Schools (NAIS), with offices located in Boston, accepts into membership any qualified independent school. This organization represents the best interests of independent schools. It promotes standards for its member schools. It champions independent schools before the Congress and before state legislatures. It is an institution of professional, academic, and scholarly societies. Its various standing committees render many services to schools and to individual teachers. Of particular value is the publication of the *Independent School Bulletin,* which carries professional articles of interest to schools and teachers at all levels of elementary and secondary education. Anyone seeking employment in an independent school should get in touch with NAIS for information essential to making a considered judgment about the desirability of teaching in any particular school.

Regional associations, where they have been organized, are also a source of information. Many large cities have associations of independent schools which do little more than hold occasional meetings. They could give factual information about a member school, but would not provide a judgment of the school's quality.

The great majority of independent schools are operated under the finest principles and standards and use their freedom with integrity. But precisely because there is no legal regulation of independent schools, and anyone is free to operate one, the better schools have stood behind the voluntary associations, such as NAIS, in order that their reputation should not be tarnished by irresponsible schools organized for purposes other than providing the best possible education for children. Membership in such associations is at least proof of a seriousness of purpose; failing to be a member does not prove a lack of integrity on the part of the school, but should cause a teacher candidate to raise the question with the school administration as to why the school is not a member.

The preceding paragraphs have given some reasons why parents might want to send their children to independent schools, but what are the reasons for wanting to teach in such schools? In general terms some of them might be the same as those given by the parents who chose this type of school for their child — a desire to teach in a school of a particular religious persuasion, a desire to teach more academically talented children than would typically be available in a public school, an interest in teaching a specialty such as music, art, ballet, or drama, the training and interest to teach children who are afflicted with a particular handicap. Usually, unless there is a specific interest, the conditions of teaching, the attitude of the administration, and the "climate" created by the goals of the school and the expectations of the families attract teachers. Salaries in most independent elementary day schools are no more than competitive with the better public schools and are often lower.

What is this "climate" that makes independent schools appeal to teachers? To describe it is not to say that all independent schools enjoy it, nor to deny that any public schools have it.

The first condition of this climate is a conviction that the best teaching and learning takes place with a relatively small number of children in each classroom. If small class size is held to, this fact is an indication that the school does indeed care about the individual child.

The second condition that is found in good independent schools is a freedom from serious disciplinary problems. Since children do not have to come to such a school and since no child has to be retained in the school, discipline problems are not created by involuntary or forced attendance. All teachers in public or independent schools must build rapport with their students, must create an atmosphere in their classrooms that is conducive to good learning. In the process of doing this there will arise certain problems of attitude and behavior which the teacher must cope with, but this is not what is meant by serious discipline problems. Serious discipline problems are time-consuming, tiring, and destructive of what a teacher would like to accomplish in class.

The third condition, which is made possible in part by the existence of the first two — small class size and co-operative students — is the freedom to innovate and experiment in curriculum and in methods of presentation. Since most independent elementary schools are small in size, communication among teachers is easy and informal. The head of the school acts usually in the capacity of a supervisor and is intimately aware of the activity and progress in each classroom.

Finally, because of their size and organization and possibly because of their very independence, policy and direction of independent schools is set to a larger extent by the faculty than is true in large public schools, where the administration must make the decisions. In good independent schools recognition of the individual voice of a teacher, making her feel she has had a part in policy formation and policy making, is an important ingredient in building teacher morale.

The decision as to whether you would be happy teaching in the somewhat "rarefied" atmosphere of an independent school as contrasted to the more "regimented" public school must be based on your nature, your interest, and what you consider to be your competencies. Basically there is no difference in teaching in one type of school or another. There are good and bad conditions to be found in almost any situation no matter how organized and operated. All children have an equal need to be taught. No one child is more precious than another. Each child's needs are different in substance and degree. Where do you feel you can function most effectively? That is the question you must answer for yourself.

8 Being a Teacher, and Some Practical Suggestions on How to Become One

You have been trained. You have been certified, but you are not yet a teacher. First some school, somewhere, will have to decide they want you. They must believe you are a good teacher, and particularly a good teacher for their school. What is a good teacher? Here are some answers taken from year-end reports of principals to their superintendents.

"She is one of those rare teachers who is quite organized and routine about her teaching, but at the same time projects a great deal of love and patient guidance into her teaching."

"The father of one of Marian's children was in the other day to discuss his daughter. The girl had a hard time in her previous grade. She is a willful child, moody and unresponsive to usual parental pressures. The father said that Marian uses magic on her children. They do what the school wants of them and more but do not feel they are being pushed in any way."

"Betty is a very strong teacher. Her children idolize her and mirror back to her the abundance of thoughtful respect that she shows to them. She had perhaps the most difficult boy in the school to handle. I suspect that no other class teacher could have handled this child while keeping the program of high quality for the rest of the class. She is careful and thorough in her work and probes deep into her subject matter with her children."

"Jane is one of our pillars. She is an excellent teacher. She knows her subject, understands her students and is a skillful inventor of teaching methods through materials. She maintains an atmosphere which makes learning not only possible but inevitable. For those students who are not reached in class, she reserves her before-school time. She is dedicated to the welfare of our school. She cares about how and where we are going and is tireless in her efforts to push the enterprise forward."

"Hilda does such a beautiful job with children that it

is difficult to remember she had not taught school before coming here. Under the quiet, smiling exterior there is a strong woman who is protective of the children in her care. She worries that we may put too much value on outgoing children. She wonders if we sometimes fail to see the potential in some of our children who are pools of quietness."

"Clare is a beautiful person in much more than a superficial sense. Seldom have I seen a teacher who combines greater sureness with modest integrity. Her leadership on the faculty was a big help and she led her group tactfully so that the work could proceed effectively."

These little highlights are about actual teachers who are in the classroom today. Even from these short sketches, it is easy to see how very different each one of these persons is. Their ages and experience range from fifty-five years old, with twenty-five years' teaching experience, to twenty-one years old, with no previous teaching experience. All of them were trained in different colleges. They come from many different states. They represent the Catholic, Protestant, and Jewish faiths. One of them happens to be a Negro and another a Chinese-Hawaian American. With different backgrounds, with diverse training and with different personalities, all of them have one thing in common — a love of children and a dedication to teaching as a profession. They are good teachers.

Elementary teachers more than teachers in any other level of education are close to their students. In nursery school, kindergarten, and the primary grades they usually have their children with them all day long. After that, specialists begin to take over in the areas of physical education, music, art, and increasingly in specialized subject fields such as mathematics, foreign language teaching and science. But even in the upper elementary grades, it is the homeroom teacher who sees the children longer than anyone else, and who thinks about the growth of the individual child, and watches the awakening of intellectual consciousness and the response to new learning.

Growth and acquisition of learning take place in other levels of education, but the amount and degree may be evident only after a long span of time — a year or even four years. With the elementary teacher, it is literally a day-by-day phenomenon. On Tuesday at 11 o'clock she sees Johnny discover what the word *growth* means. He has planted a seed in the classroom flower pot and now he sees it sprouting from the ground, the beginnings of a flower. Or he has watched the two mice, one of whom was being fed very nutritious foods and the other a minimum diet. Suddenly the word *growth* appears in his reading book and he knows what it means in the story. He relates it to the seed and to the mouse and then he thinks about himself! This realization, this awakening that can be seen in the face of a child is what an elementary teacher experiences hourly in her classroom.

Every teacher knows that no two of her students are alike. Each is an individual, each learns at a different rate, each is sensitive to different experiences, and each is affected by outside influences that vary as greatly as anything within themselves.

Just as students vary and are different one from the other, teachers too are different one from the other, but they have a common bond in their love of children, in their love of teaching, and in their belief in the teaching profession. As personalities they are individuals, unique, with certain strengths and with certain weaknesses. For that reason it is very important to understand that there are many and varied ways of fulfilling and satisfying one's love of children and one's desire to teach. Not every type of classroom or school district is right for every teacher. The very first responsibility of anyone thinking about teaching is to think about himself. Ask yourself, what am I really like? What are the things I really love to do? What are the things I'm afraid of?

There are so many different and varied opportunities in elementary teaching that it would be a shame if you found yourself teaching in a situation which did not suit you and therefore you decided you did not like teaching. It might well be that you are potentially an excellent teacher but under different circumstances. For instance, the teacher who is extremely successful with academically talented youngsters who come from rich cultural backgrounds might be a very poor teacher in a culturally deprived area of one of our big cities. Or the teacher who is most successful in the one elementary school of a small rural town might be totally inadequate in a classroom of a county-wide school for the physically handicapped. Or to take something even more basic, the demands on a nursery school teacher are in many ways quite different from those on the elementary science specialist who deals with fourth, fifth, and six graders. Despite these differences of interests, all are elementary teachers with the same basic beliefs and feelings.

But you still have to be hired to have a chance to be a teacher!

The first interview for a position in a public school district is often rather frightening. Of course, many questions will be asked, and properly so, and you will be judged, in part at least, by how you respond to these questions. Your school and college record and the recommendations that have been written for you will probably weigh much more heavily than the personal interview, but the personal interview is important and you should go to it prepared to be as straight-forward and direct as possible. Never be afraid to say, "I don't know," for the chances are the person asking you the question doesn't know either and raises the question more to see how you will handle it than to receive an answer.

Your appearance is important, but do not over-dress because this is very obvious to an experienced interviewer. On the other hand, your dress is one indication of what teaching means to you and what you believe a teacher is. If you are "flashy" in appearance, that is one implied conception. If you look dowdy or frumpy, that too expresses an idea. In short, be yourself, be as natural as you possibly can be so that what you bring to an interview is exactly what you intend to bring every day to your school and to your class.

You should be thinking about the other side of an interview. What questions should you be asking? You will gain a certain judgment of the kind of district represented by the interviewer by the manner in which the interview is conducted. If it is perfunctory, superficial and shallow, the chances are this represents the attitude of the district or at least of its administration. If the interviewer, on the other hand, avoids asking questions about information he already has on your application blank or in your transcripts, but asks you about your attitudes and your opinions, then there is reason to hope that this more serious-minded attitude reflects the attitude of the district. From either side of the interview table, however, because of the shortness of time involved, an interview should never be given too much weight. An interview is one aspect of the evidence for you to judge. A good interviewer will consider it as such and you, the interviewed, should also treat the occasion in that manner.

First of all, you must decide what type of district will best suit your personality. In other words, in what sort of district will you be comfortable and free to grow and develop professionally as you would like. There are tremendous differences between school districts. The small rural district has an attitude about education, shown in the way it conducts its schools and the way it fits into the community, which is very different from the large city school district. The suburban middle class district has many problems that are different from those of the culturally deprived sub-district of a big city. You must decide the kind of community that you wish to live in. You must decide to what aspect of public education you believe you can contribute to the greatest degree with your particular talents, with your particular interests and with your particular limitations. Before even going to your first interview, you should have attempted to think through as clearly as possible what you should be looking for and what you need to fulfill your hopes of being a successful teacher.

Once in the interview you can gain considerable insight into the attitude of the district that is interviewing you by asking them questions about their average class size. At what point does the district set up new elementary class sections? What number of children is considered tolerable in any given class? If they divide a section when it reaches thirty, that can be considered good. If they divide their sections when they reach forty or fifty, you are in an overcrowded situation and the district is cutting corners in order to economize.

For elementary teachers it is particularly important to know how much time each day the school district requires a teacher to be with her children in the classroom. Some states have regulations which specify how many minutes per day a teacher is expected to have as free time. Many districts give teachers a period a day on their own by having specialists in physical education take their classes. Specialists in music or in art, or in some subject matter area — foreign languages, science, mathematics — often take over the class, but in these instances it is better if the homeroom teacher stays to observe.

Lunch hour and recess obligations are important to know about for they too express quite clearly a district's attitude about the value of the professional training of a teacher. Is every day lunchroom attendance considered by the district more important than freedom for the teacher? Does the district expect a homeroom teacher to collect lunch money? Is the homeroom teacher expected to collect money for a banking program? What kind of attendance records are required? Who weighs the children and keeps the chart? In short, how much pure clerical work is a teacher expected to do? There is always some clerical work required of all teachers, but those school districts which attempt to reduce this kind of activity by teachers to the minimum are saying by their actions that they believe the professional training of the teacher is so valuable that it should be protected from nonprofessional, time-consuming chores. The attitude of a school district about class size, the required time to be spent in the class, and the type of duties other than teaching expected of the teacher will reveal a great deal about the kind of district it is and its educational goals.

Another question that should be asked concerns the attitude of the district about in-service training of their teachers. Is orientation time set aside before the school year opens? Are workshops promoted during the school year or between semesters? Planned activities of this kind not only upgrade a district totally, but benefit each teacher and make him a far more effective and valuable person in the classroom. Further, the fact that a district will take the time, effort, and money to organize in-service training is another clear indication of its seriousness of purpose.

Summer programs and sabbatical leaves will also reveal the degree of commitment with which the district accepts its obligations to upgrade the professional quality of its faculty. Does the district encourage summer study by underwriting in whole or in part courses taken at university summer schools? What kind of encouragement does the district give to its faculty members to apply for National Science Foundation grants in the sciences, mathematics, and foreign languages? What kind of encouragement does it give to its faculty to attend National Defense Education Act institutes in the humanities? Elementary teachers have many opportunities to receive grants of this kind, but they should be encouraged by their districts and advised as to which would be the most profitable to the individual and to the district. Policies on sabbatical leaves for public school districts are gradually being adopted. The more enlightened districts have developed specific policies; others have a permissive type of policy which they can apply in particular cases. And there are still districts which do not have any policy about sabbatical leaves and do not intend to have sabbatical leaves granted to their teachers.

Ask what the school district's attitude is toward exchange of teachers within the United States and with foreign lands. After one has taught for five years or more, exchanging with a foreign teacher, for instance, can be extraordinarily stimulating to the individual and beneficial in the long run to the district. In this same connection, does the district have any policy about leaves of absence which would permit a teacher to go to one of our service schools run by the armed forces in many parts of the world?

Does a school district have a professional library for its faculty? Where is it located? How is it staffed? How large is it? And what manner of service does it provide the teacher? A professional library in a school district is one of the least expensive resources the district can maintain and yet can be one of the most helpful and beneficial "in-service" factors for teachers. Not only should such a library have the latest professional books, and books related to teaching, but it should also provide a good selection of professional journals. The professional library, if the community has a good library, or if there are college or university libraries in the neighborhood, can have co-operative services available for loans and exchanges.

In asking these questions, you do not expect any one school district to have all these opportunities for teachers, but the plans they do have available express an attitude about enriching experiences for their teachers which will be significant in helping you judge the district. Your attitude and seriousness about teaching is revealed to your interviewer by the nature of your questions. Both sides are making judgments, and it is proper that they should.

Another important series of questions that a candidate should ask concerns the school district's and the community's attitude toward PTA meetings. Beware of the district which does not encourage PTA meetings at regularly scheduled times, for it will be a district which either cares little for parents' opinions about the education of their children or fears to have the parents express their opinions. Successful education of children at the elementary level must combine the efforts of the administrators of the school district, the teachers in the classrooms, the children, and their parents. If any one of these four elements is left out, the child's education will suffer. It is never possible to get a perfect balance among these four elements, but it is essential that all four be present at all times. If a community's school district relationship is so uneasy that PTA meetings cannot be profitable, then you can be almost certain that the quality of education in this district will not be very high.

Many districts will answer teaching candidates' questions by producing policy handbooks which probably are the results of cooperative efforts on the part of the administration and the teachers, with the final approval of the school board. One policy, for instance, which reveals a great deal about a district's attitude toward its teachers concerns absences due to sickness. There are districts which spell out in great detail the number of days that a teacher is permitted to be absent because of illness. Any days beyond that are charged against the teacher's salary. At the other end of the spectrum are the districts which say if a teacher is sick, he should obviously stay home until he is well. The latter district treats each teacher as a fully qualified professional with integrity, who is not going to take advantage of this type of ruling. It is ironic that in many instances districts of the first kind, which spell out the number of days "allowed," find teachers "saving up" and taking holidays with the time remaining on their permitted sick leaves. Whereas districts with no sick leave accounting will find teachers coming to school when they probably should be home in bed! The only instances where the policy might not reveal the attitude of the district would be in very large urban school districts, which must be impersonal because of the number of teachers, many of them temporary or substitutes. In these large districts with literally thousands of teachers, the financial aspects of an open policy could lead to unnecessary waste and confusion. On the other hand, in districts of normal size, the administration should be able to judge whether or not teachers are suitable from a professional point of view and hire and retain them on that basis. The type of person who will take advantage of open sick leave is obviously not suitable to be a teacher.

The matter of sick leave has been stressed only as another example of the attitude of a school district toward its faculty. A policy handbook will reveal a great deal in this respect. Is the teacher considered as a professional? As a person with integrity? What, if anything, is said in the policy handbook about the personal appearance of the teacher? About her mode of dress? Are there statements about social conduct, about smoking, about drinking? There are still public schools in the United States which specify that teachers may not wear any form of makeup, may not smoke or drink in public. Such regulations say a good deal about the community and the community's attitude towards teachers. A community has a right to any attitude it cares to assume, but you, the candidate, should be aware of its beliefs before you make your decision. Do the regulations in the handbook, in your judgment, promote the dignity of the individual teacher and the value of the profession? If these questions can be answered in the affirmative, it is a good sign. If the regulations seem to be designed on a basis of mistrust and suspicion, this would say a good deal on the negative side in judging that district.

Now we come to a matter of great importance to candidates for teaching positions which unfortunately is a question that is not easy to answer. What is the social attitude of the community? An indication as has been suggested will be found in the regulations and policies of the school district. Furthermore, what is a socially acceptable attitude? The answer to this is a very personal one. What might be completely tolerable to you could be totally intolerable to another. Certainly you can ask whether the community and the school district are integrated ethnically, religiously, and socially. If they are not, it might be well, if the thought of segregation makes you uncomfortable, to ask why such conditions exist.

If you and your family have always been either Republicans or Democrats politically, a community in which the majority were of the opposite persuasion might be a concern to you.

Even more subtle and difficult to evaluate is the accepted moral behavior standard of the community. What follows is an actual defense made by a teacher before a school board for having taught a certain book. An anonymous telephone call had come to Miss Eleanor C. Parker, who was teaching English in Laconia, New Hampshire, taking her to task for having taught Harper Lee's *To Kill A Mockingbird*. Fortunately, because it is a small town, the man who made the anonymous call was located and was asked to appear at a school board meeting so that he and Miss Parker might publicly discuss the issue. The fundamental questions involved were what was the school board's (and one can assume the community's) attitude about the freedom of a teacher in her classroom, and what was the level of tolerance in this community.

As part of the statement she prepared, Miss Parker wrote:

I love to teach. I have spent over half my life working with young people in school and in church, and working with language, the miracle that makes us human. It is through language that we think, communicate, express our ideas, and transmit them down the years. Why study literature? Because it is one of the humanities — one of the ways by which man expresses his beliefs, his hopes, his understandings. The study of literature helps us to develop understanding of ourselves and others without having to experience directly every aspect of life. It helps us to develop critical judgment of good and poor expression, logical and illogical thought, even truth and untruth. It helps us to develop responsibility as individuals, members of families, citizens. It helps us to develop values, ideals, a sense of purpose, an understanding of what life is all about. I consider the book *To Kill A Mockingbird* a superior resource for such development because the basic idea of the book is that prejudice poisons the mind, and that the only cure is understanding.

The school board voted unanimously to support Miss Parker. Mr. X did not represent the level of tolerance of the community of Laconia. Miss Parker then knew where she stood on such issues. It is well for anyone about to enter teaching to be able to answer the question the class asked Miss Parker, "What happens if we are told we cannot continue to discuss this book?" What value do you place on the dignity of a teacher? On your integrity as a person?

No mention has been made so far about salaries, and for a good reason. Salary schedules in public schools are usually published and are known to all. Beginning salaries between similar school districts vary comparatively little. Size and region of the country have an effect, but then so does the cost of living vary between city, town, and country. "Take-home pay" after room and board can be more important than the total amount of salary. Given a reasonable salary scale, the important questions to ask concerning salary are how the increases are organized, on what basis are these increments given, and on what basis has the salary schedule been set up. Is there a combination of longevity, advanced degrees, and credit hours? Is there an element of merit involved in the salary schedule? And if so, how is that merit administered and decided upon?

The so-called extra benefits or fringe benefits are sometimes important, particularly when they involve health insurance, accident insurance, and life insurance. Ask about the retirement plan. Is it locally run or is it run by the state? How much does the individual contribute and how much does the district contribute? Is social security involved or not? Understand the actual nature of the formal contract. There are many different state rulings on forms of contract. In some states, if new contracts have not been issued by a certain date, the teacher is automatically rehired for the following year. In certain states no contract is issued until the tax levy has been passed by the voting public. In other states it is specified exactly what area the teacher will be teaching and there can be no deviation from this on the part of the school district. Other regulations permit a very broad type of contract arrangement which could mean that a teacher would be asked to take classes in areas in which he really did not feel totally competent to teach. Some districts and states have tenure laws, that is to say after a certain number of years, usually between three and five, the teacher cannot be dismissed except for some serious moral charge. Sometimes tenure regulations are of local creation and vary between districts within a state. Sometimes they are state laws. It is not so much a question of whether or not tenure is a good thing as it is a question of knowing what the regulations are that concern you directly, if you are employed by a given district.

To sum up this whole matter of the practical side of things, it should be evident that a candidate has two main concerns: (1) Know yourself. What attitude about education will you accept? What attitude about education will bring out the best that is in you? What "climate" of opinion, belief, and ethical standards will you be comfortable with? (2) Does the district fulfill the expectations you have set for yourself and for it? Does it have high professional standards and integrity? If by the questions you have been asked and by the answers to questions you in turn have asked the district you feel reasonably confident that you would be content and eager to be hired as a teacher, you have done all you can, at this stage. The next step will be to find out, at whatever level you have chosen, whether or not you truly are a teacher!

You have been hired, but you are not yet a teacher. What is it to be a teacher? What is good teaching? The protest of a good teacher, Patrick Bratton of Long Beach, California, to a mythical Miss Kaplan, who is not yet a good teacher, will suggest what good teaching is not!

(A first grade student said, "Spring is a long day." "You

mean, 'In Spring the days are long,'" Miss Kaplan, the teacher, said.)

Song on a Spring Day to Miss K.

"Spring is a long day"
Is doubtless not the way
That Fun with Dick and Jane
Would say that lengthening light
Is children's great delight
In seeing end of winter's numbing pain.

But, dear Miss Kaplan, we
Prosaic souls must be
Who dare to call it wrong.
For "Spring's a long day"
May be a poet's way
To sing the thought, "In Spring the days are long."

For Spring is a long day
When your aim is play
And buds are bursting wild.
And Spring is running fast
Or rolling in the grass,
For even tulips smile — when you're a child!

Good teaching is "hearing" the child, listening, and understanding. Miss Kaplan did not hear, listen, or understand.

When you are a good teacher, what are your satisfactions? Dr. Philip Jackson of the University of Chicago asked a number of teachers this same question and recorded their answers on tape. One suburban teacher put it this way:

> "I think it's kind of like missionary work. I've always been very socially-minded, and I think that we really do have a lot of work to do right in these communities, not just in the underprivileged — the other too."

Another teacher was particularly excited by the fact that at the elementary level you are dealing with children at the most critical age of their lives:

> "Well, I think when you're helping young people, and — You're teaching them something new all the time, you're helping them to develop, especially down at this age, if they do not get a good background — this is my feeling anyway . . . I feel that if they do not have a good background by the time they come out of second grade, that they will have trouble going on."

Proceeding with his interviews, Dr. Jackson recorded the following:

> "Let's see, the rewards. I think just seeing them happy and seeing them progress is the biggest reward. . . . Seeing a child be successful. I think this is the thing we are striving for, really, in education. We want to see a child find his place in life and be successful, and when he's on

the road to this, even in school — we watch. At least I do; I watch my youngsters as they go along and progress. I check up with the fourth grade teachers and see whether or not there are strengths or weaknesses or things that I should have been doing with them to help them along the way."

"Well, progress for one thing. I mean I try to keep a very close check on how they're getting along. I feel that if I have a child that comes in the fall and has many problems, many difficulties, and he overcomes some of them, then I feel that we're making progress, and we're getting someplace."

One summed it up in this sentence, "I get a bang out of seeing their faces light up with an idea, or a sense of accomplishment."

Teachers who love their work in their daily lives try to express their sense of excitement. One teacher in these series of interviews by Dr. Jackson got pretty close to the heart of it:

"I just wish that everyone could feel the excitement that there is in teaching — the eagerness to get into the classroom. And it's the strangest thing, I'm sure that you must feel it too, even on your level, that no matter if you're sad or if you don't feel well or you know, even if things aren't the rosiest, you can come in in the morning and someone will come up, and it's gone. All of a sudden if he's sad, if the child is sad, you forget, you know. Because either you're needed or maybe a child has come in with something they just have to tell you, and it's just the biggest thing in the world. And all of a sudden, you forget. And I just wonder if there are other occupations like this, where people find the same gratification."

Contributing to the excitement are the surprises:

"Oh, well, I've mentioned some of them. Class discussion, that veers in a surprising direction, where you never thought it'd go. And it goes higher than you ever dreamed possible. A child who will — for example, who had never had any ideas that showed, and suddenly makes an observation, brings two things together: 'That's just like this.' Well, sometimes it's joy from one kid who suddenly made a spurt and did something that you never thought he could do. Sometimes it's a whole class that does something together that you never thought a class could do . . . A little girl one year, in the fifth grade, after class one day she came up and she said, 'I just learned how to divide.' That was that day — it was that class period, I don't know how it happened, but it happened."

"Let me cite one case specifically where a child did a series of triangles and thought it was beautiful, and it wasn't beautiful. So I asked her to use her eyes and observe and see if she could make it better, and she was quite agreeable to looking out the window and looking at the forms that windows make, and looking at the forms that a building makes, and we worked on her drawing.

I don't think I've ever seen a more thrilled face than when she realized that she could do something to make it more interesting. She sort of became uncorked."

"It's also the successes you've had — when you've had, say, a child that's been a real severe problem and some way you've reached him and you've done something for him. And I just don't think there's any job that has the depth of feeling that you have in a situation like this. Oh, perhaps a doctor, when he saves a life or something. But I think in most professions, they don't have — well, it's almost a spiritual thing that you get when you've had a success reaching a child or helping him."

When you can hear, listen to, and understand each child in your class, you have become a good teacher. And when you are a good teacher, you will have the satisfactions that these experienced teachers reported to Dr. Jackson.

9 The Opportunity, the Privilege

Emily Dickinson once asked the question:

Could you tell me
How to grow
Or is it unconveyed,
Like melody or witchcraft?

Will anyone ever know? Can anyone ever be sure that he is helping a child to grow? We all know that growth occurs, but surprisingly little is known about how it takes place. We believe that to grow in the fullest sense of the term an individual must learn. But then we ask, what is the nature of learning? Scholars have pondered this question for centuries. Socrates, Plato, Bacon, Newton, Dewey are among the educational philosophers who have attempted to find an answer.

Most experienced teachers conclude that, given the necessary knowledge and skills, a teacher does best who has love, concern, and understanding for the individual child. Knowledge and skills enable the teacher to interpret better what is before him, to anticipate sooner what may develop, to prepare more meaningful guidelines that will help. But all this knowledge and all these skills have little effect unless the love and concern of the teacher is conveyed to the child. Here is a story from a different context to bring this fact home:

Bob Wiley had been in the penitentiary for the past five years serving out a sentence for armed robbery. He came from a small rural town that was little more than a water stop on the trunk line of one of the major railroads. His widowed mother still lived in the little house whose backyard extended right up to the railroad tracks. The house was about a half mile up the tracks from the whistle stop.

Bob had informed his mother by postal card the date of his release. He had not said whether he was coming home or not. He could not decide whether his being home would hurt his mother. In this little town everyone knew everyone else and he was the first one from there ever to "serve time." Perhaps his presence and the explanations she would have to make would be too painful for her. Nevertheless he could not resist taking the train that would go right by his house. His "old man" had worked for the railroads until he had been killed in a coupling accident. Bob could remember as a boy the excitement in the house when his father was due back after a stint working a long haul freight. His mother used to put up some kind of welcoming sign in the backyard.

Another "ex-con" who had been let out with Bob was with him on the train. As they got nearer his home town, Bob grew more and more nervous and fidgety. He turned to his companion and said, "Jim, in a few minutes you're going to see a little house by the tracks with a backyard. Jim, as soon as you spot the house, tell me what you see."

"What I see? What do you mean, Bob?"

"Describe the house and the yard. It's mighty important to me, Jim."

Jim peered out the window and soon said, "Has the house got one chimney, dead center on the roof?"

"Yeah, that's right."

"There seem to be two windows and a door giving out on the yard."

"That's it."

"The yard has a little wooden fence around it."

"Jim, is there a tree in the middle of the yard?"

"Yeah, right in the middle and Bob . . ." By that time they were practically opposite the house.

"Bob, the damndest thing, the tree is all covered with red ribbons!"

Bob got off at the whistle stop. To him a sign had been given, a love was being expressed.

There is nowhere in the whole range of education where a "sign" is more clearly understood or responded to than at the elementary level. Children at this age see clearly. Their vision has not been obscured by fears, doubts, and cynicisms. As a teacher in the elementary grades you have the opportunity to hang out the sign that will encourage learning, stimulate thought, and promote growth. We may not know how learning or growth takes place, but we do know what conditions encourage learning, and what climate nurtures growth.

Whether you choose to teach in a big city, in the suburbs, or in a rural area, whether you choose to teach in an armed forces dependency school overseas, in a Peace Corps school in Africa, or in a missionary school in some remote corner of the world, the opportunity remains the same.

Whatever grade level you choose, whatever specialty you select, the basic challenge for every teacher, as it will be for you, is how best to reach the child so that he can be guided, helped, and encouraged to learn and to grow as a whole person, secure, with ideals and standards that will hold up under strain and stress.

In the world today there are an infinite number of

choices for people in deciding what they want to do for a life's work. Many jobs and professions require a maximum of technical skill and a minimum of dealing with other human beings. There are many fine people who feel threatened when dealing with children. Youth seems to challenge their knowledge, their authority, their position as adults, whereas if they deal with computer machines, using the skill and technical knowledge that is required, their satisfaction in knowing they are doing a difficult job well reassures them and gives them happiness. Their relationship with their own age group is on a basis of equality. Not all people have outgoing personalities, fortunately. Some are shy, some like action better than contemplation. None of these characteristics indicate a good or a bad person. They simply indicate the kind of person.

Before you decide to teach, think about yourself. Do you love children? Would you be interested in working with them? If you don't know, find out by baby-sitting, working in a summer camp, being a cadet teacher at your high school, working in playgrounds or summer recreation programs. There are an infinite number of ways to test yourself. If you decide you would not like teaching, after a fair trial, this is a sensible decision for you and is in no way a criticism of your character.

There is a reason far greater than selfish interest why young people who are considering teaching must think about its demands and responsibilities. As teachers they will deal with other people's lives. The elementary teacher will be dealing with children when they begin to form their characters as thinking, sensitive persons. A bad teacher at the college level is hardly more than irritating and frustrating to a student. A bad teacher at the elementary level can affect the whole future of a child. The satisfactions of being an elementary teacher are infinite, but the responsibilities are awesome.

Children ask the basic questions that face us all — who am I? Why am I here? Where did I come from? Where am I going? Who are you? What kind of a world is this? In elementary school the questions, never phrased as simply as this, are asked for the first time. You, as an elementary school teacher, will have the opportunity to help your students find answers that lead them toward knowledge and wisdom. Do you wish to take advantage of such an opportunity? It is a privilege to do so. Good luck.

Acknowledgments

To ACKNOWLEDGE the help that has been received in the writing of this book, I must go back and thank the many and long-suffering students who have had me as a teacher since the fall of 1933. Next on the list in "preparing" me as an author are the teachers who had me as a student, most especially Arthur Peaslee, Hewitt Reynolds, Margery Bailey, Hank Blagden, C. S. Lewis, William Burton, Alfred Simpson, Robert Ulich, and Charles Lee. Then my gratitude goes to that wonderful group of colleagues that it has been my good fortune to associate with at the Deane School, St. Paul's School, Harvard University, the Clayton, Missouri, Public School District, and the Laboratory Schools of the University of Chicago.

More specifically I want to thank for their contributions to the Bibliography and in certain instances for their permission to quote from their own written materials: Professor Robert H. Anderson of Harvard, Miss Rose Bello of the Laboratory Schools of the University of Chicago, Professor Bruno Bettelheim, Director of the Orthogenic School of the University of Chicago, Mrs. Lonnie Carton of Tufts University, Professor Morris L. Cogan of the University of Pittsburgh, Professor William Fowler, formerly Principal of the Nursery School of the University of Chicago, Professor Philip Jackson of the University of Chicago, Professor Daniel A. Marshall of Tufts University, Professor Robert Newman of Syracuse University, Miss Louise Pliss of the Laboratory Schools of the University of Chicago, Dean Robert J. Schaefer of Teachers College, Columbia University, Professor Herbert A. Thelen of the University of Chicago, and Dr. Morvin A. Wirtz, Director of the Division of Handicapped Children and Youth of the United States Office of Education.

To transcribe my particular and peculiar intonations from tapes, and then to put my written words into final form was the task that Victoria Kokoras cheerfully undertook from the hesitant beginnings to the happy ending. For her ingenuity, skill, and optimism I am indeed grateful.

Bibliography
For Those Who Wish to Read in Depth

CURRICULUM (General)

Benjamin, H. *The Saber-Tooth Curriculum* (New York: McGraw-Hill, 1939).

Dewey, J. *The Child and the Curriculum* (Chicago: Phoenix Books, University of Chicago Press, 1962).

Goodlad, J. I., and Anderson, R. H. *The Nongraded Elementary School* (New York: Harcourt, Brace, 1963).

Montessori, Maria. *The Montessori Method* (New York: Schocken Books, 1964).

Tyler, R. *Basic Principles of Curriculum Instruction.* (Chicago: University of Chicago Press, 1950).

EXCEPTIONAL CHILD

Bettelheim, B. *Love is Not Enough: the Treatment of Emotionally Disturbed Children* (Glencoe, Illinois: Free Press, 1950).

Cruickshank, W. M. *Psychology of Exceptional Children and Youth* (New York: Prentice-Hall, 1951).

Getzels, J., and Jackson, P. *Creativity and Intelligence: Explorations with Gifted Students* (New York: Wiley, 1962).

Kirk, Samuel. *Educating Exceptional Children* (Boston: Houghton Mifflin, 1962).

Redl, F., and Wineman, D. *The Aggressive Child* (Glencoe, Ill.: Free Press, 1957).

GENERAL: FICTION

Ashton-Warner, S. *Spinster* (New York: Simon & Schuster, 1959).

Ashton-Warner, S. *The Teacher* (New York, Simon & Schuster, 1963).

Bjørneboe, Jens. *The Least of These.* (New York: Bobbs-Merrill, 1959).

Hersey, J. *The Child Buyer* (New York: Alfred A. Knopf, 1960).

Kaufman, B. *Up the Down Staircase* (Englewood Cliffs, N.J.: Prentice-Hall, 1964).

GENERAL: PROFESSIONAL

Bettelheim, B. *The Informed Heart: Autonomy in a Mass Age* (Glencoe, Ill.: Free Press, 1960).

Erikson, Erik H. *Childhood and Society* (New York: Norton, 1963).

Havighurst, R. *Human Development and Education* (New York: Longmans, Green, 1953).

Mead, Margaret. *The School in American Culture* (Cambridge: Harvard University Press, 1951).

Whitehead, A. *The Aims of Education* (New York: Mentor Books, New American Library, 1963).

HISTORY AND PHILOSOPHY

Cremin, L. A. *The Transformation of the Schools* (New York: Alfred A. Knopf, 1955).

Dewey, J. *Experience and Education* (New York: Collier Books, 1963).

Harvard Committee. *General Education in a Free Society* (Cambridge: Harvard University Press, 1945).

Phenix, P. H. *Philosophy of Education* (New York: Holt, 1958).

Ulich, R. *History of Educational Thought* (New York: American Book Co., 1945).

JOURNALS (Professional — General)

Child Development (Society for Research in Child Development, University of Chicago Press).

Childhood Education (Association of Childhood Development, 3615 Wisconsin Avenue, Washington, D.C.).

The Elementary School Journal (University of Chicago Press).

The Independent School Bulletin (National Association of Independent Schools, 4 Liberty Square, Boston, Mass.).

NEA Journal (National Education Association, 1201 Sixteenth Street, N.W., Washington, D.C.).

INDEPENDENT SCHOOLS

Chamberlain, E. *Our Independent Schools* (New York: American Book Co., 1944).

Heely, A. *Why the Private School?* (New York: Harper, 1951).

Mallery, D. *New Approaches in Education* (National Association of Independent Schools, 4 Liberty Square, Boston, Mass.).

USEFUL REFERENCE BOOKS

Encyclopedia of Educational Research (New York: Macmillan, 1960).

Handbook of Private Schools, 46th edition (Boston: Porter Sargent, 1965).

College Blue Books, 11th edition (New York, 1965).

Redefer, F., and Reeves, D. *Careers in Education* (New York: Harper, 1960).

Teaching as a Career (Washington, D. C.: Office of Education, 1965).

SPECIALISTS

ART

Johnson, P. "Art for the Young Child," Chap. IV, 64th Yearbook, N.S.S.E. (Chicago: University of Chicago Press, 1965).

Read, H. *Education Through Art* (New York: Random House, 1956).

FOREIGN LANGUAGES

Andersson, T. *The Teaching of Foreign Languages in the Elementary School* (Boston: Heath, 1953).

Dunkel, H., and Pillet, R. *French in the Elementary School* (Chicago: University of Chicago Press, 1962).

GUIDANCE

Nitzschke, D., and Hill, G. *The Elementary School Counselor: Preparation and Functions* (Ohio University, Pupil Service Series, 1964).

Rogers, D. *Mental Hygiene in Elementary Education* (Boston: Houghton Mifflin, 1957).

MATHEMATICS

Dienes, Z. P. *Building Up Mathematics* (London: Hutchinson, 1960).

Goutard, M. *Mathematics and Children* (Reading, England: Educational Explorers, Ltd., 1964).

MUSIC

Myers, L. *Teaching Children Music in the Elementary School* (Englewood Cliffs, N.J.: Prentice-Hall, 1961).

Swanson, B. *Music in the Education of Children* (San Francisco: Wadsworth, 1961).

PHYSICAL EDUCATION

Halsey, E., and Porter, L. *Physical Education for Children* (New York: Holt, 1963).

Murray, R. *Dance in Elementary Education* (New York: Harper, 1963).

READING AND THE LANGUAGE ARTS

Austin, M., and Morrison, C. *The First R: The Harvard Report on Reading in Elementary Schools* (New York: Macmillan, 1963).

Downing, J. *The Initial Teaching Alphabet* (London: University of London, 1964).

SCIENCE

Podendorf, I. *Discovering Science on Your Own* (New York: Grosset & Dunlap, 1962).

Schwab, J., and Brandwein, P. *The Teaching of Science* (Cambridge: Harvard University Press, 1962).

SOCIAL STUDIES

Wesley, E., and Adams, M. *Teaching Social Studies in Elementary Schools* (Boston: Heath, 1952).

Willcockson, Mary. *Social Education of Young Children: Kindergarten, Primary Grades* (Washington, D.C.: National Council for the Social Studies, 1956).

SPEECH THERAPIST

Battin, R., and Hang, C. *Speech and Language Delay* (Springfield, Ill.: Thomas, 1964).

Hejna, R. *Speech Disorders and Non-Directive Therapy* (New York: Ronald Press, 1960).

Appendix A
Elementary MAT Programs

COLLEGES AND UNIVERSITIES OFFERING PROGRAMS THAT
LEAD TO THE DEGREE OF MASTER OF ARTS IN TEACHING
(MAT) AT THE ELEMENTARY LEVEL, OR MASTER OF SCIENCE
IN TEACHING (MST)

California

LaVerne College, LaVerne
Stanford University, Palo Alto
University of Redlands, Redlands
University of San Francisco

Colorado

Colorado College, Colorado Springs

Connecticut

University of Hartford

District of Columbia

George Washington University

Florida

Rollins College, Winter Park

Georgia

Emory University, Atlanta

Illinois

Chicago Teachers College, South Chicago

Rockford College, Rockford
University of Chicago, Chicago

Indiana

DePauw University, Greencastle

Massachusetts

Harvard University, Cambridge
University of Massachusetts, Amherst

Michigan

Siena Heights College, Adrian

Missouri

Washington University, St. Louis
Webster College, Webster Groves

Nebraska

Wayne State College, Wayne

New Jersey

Glassboro State College, Glassboro
Trenton State College, Trenton

New Mexico

New Mexico State University, University Park

Ohio

Oberlin College, Oberlin

Oklahoma

Oklahoma City University

Oregon

Lewis and Clark College, Portland
Portland State College

Rhode Island

Brown University, Providence
Rhode Island College, Providence

South Carolina

Winthrop College, Rock Hill

South Dakota

Augustana College, Sioux Falls
Northern State College, Aberdeen

Texas

Texas Woman's University, Denton

Washington

Walla Walla College, College Place

Appendix B

Elementary Guidance Programs

COLLEGES AND UNIVERSITIES OFFERING "DISTINCTIVELY
DIFFERENT" PROGRAMS IN ELEMENTARY SCHOOL GUIDANCE

Alabama

University of Alabama, University

Arizona

Arizona State College, Flagstaff

California

San Diego State College

San Jose State College

Sacramento State College

Delaware

University of Delaware, Newark

Hawaii

University of Hawaii, Honolulu

Illinois

University of Illinois, Urbana

National College of Education, Evanston

Rockford College, Rockford

Indiana

Purdue University, Lafayette

Iowa

State College of Iowa, Cedar Falls

Kansas

Fort Hays Kansas State College
Kansas State Teachers College, Emporia
University of Kansas, Lawrence
Kansas State College of Pittsburg

Missouri

University of Missouri at Kansas City
Saint Louis University
Washington University, St. Louis
University of Missouri, Columbia
Central Missouri State College, Warrensburg
Northeast Missouri State Teachers College, Kirksville

Massachusetts

Boston College

New York

Bank Street College of Education, New York City
New York University, New York City
Long Island University, Brooklyn
Teachers College, Columbia University, New York City
Yeshiva University, New York City

Ohio

Ohio University, Athens

Oklahoma

East Central State College, Ada
Oklahoma State University, Stillwater

Oregon

Oregon State University, Corvallis

University of Oregon, Eugene

University of Portland

Pennsylvania

Bryn Mawr College, Bryn Mawr

Pennsylvania State University, University
  Park

Rhode Island

Rhode Island College, Providence

Texas

Texas Western College, El Paso

North Texas State University, Denton

Wyoming

University of Wyoming, Laramie

Index